MIXED-MEDIA BOOKS

MIXED-MEDIA BOOKS
Dozens of Experiments in Altering Books

Gabe Cyr

LARK BOOKS

A Division of Sterling Publishing Co., Inc.
New York / London

EDITORS: Meg Greene Malvasi, Deborah Morgenthal, Jane Woodsides • ASSOCIATE EDITORS: Rebecca Guthrie, Nathalie Mornu, Susan Kieffer
ART DIRECTOR: 828, Inc. • COVER DESIGNER: Barbara Zaretsky • ASSOCIATE ART DIRECTOR: Shannon Yokeley
ART PRODUCTION ASSISTANT: Jeff Hamilton • EDITORIAL ASSISTANCE: Delores Gosnell, Dawn Dillingham
ILLUSTRATOR: Katherine Shaughnessy • CHAPTER OPENER ART: Sheila Longo Petruccelli • PHOTOGRAPHER: Steve Mann
EDITORIAL INTERNS: David L. Squires, Sue Stigleman

The Library of Congress has cataloged the hardcover edition as follows:

Cyr, Gabe, 1943-
  New directions in altered books / Gabe Cyr.
      p. cm.
  Includes index.
  ISBN 1-57990-694-X (hardcover)
  1. Altered books. I. Title.

  TT896.3.C87 2006
  702'.8'1--dc22

                              2005037052

10 9 8 7 6 5 4 3 2 1

Published by Lark Books, A Division of
Sterling Publishing Co., Inc.
387 Park Avenue South, New York, N.Y. 10016

First Paperback Edition 2009

Previously published as New Directions in Altered Books

Distributed in Canada by Sterling Publishing,
c/o Canadian Manda Group, 165 Dufferin Street
Toronto, Ontario, Canada M6K 3H6

Distributed in the United Kingdom by GMC Distribution Services,
Castle Place, 166 High Street, Lewes, East Sussex, England BN7 1XU

Distributed in Australia by Capricorn Link (Australia) Pty Ltd.,
P.O. Box 704, Windsor, NSW 2756 Australia

If you have questions or comments about this book, please contact:
Lark Books
67 Broadway
Asheville, NC 28801
(828) 253-0467

Manufactured in China

ISBN 13: 978-1-57990-694-8 (hardcover) 978-1-60059-543-1 (paperback)

For information about custom editions, special sales, premium and corporate purchases, please contact Sterling Special Sales Department at 800-805-5489 or specialsales@sterlingpub.com.

TABLE OF CONTENTS

INGRID DIJKERS
Flight, 2005
Small book, wood, papier mâché, soft butterfly body sewn to book binding, marabou feathers; structurally-altered book turned into a free-standing sculpture, bead embellishment

INTRODUCTION

MY PASSION IN LIFE IS ABOUT CREATING things and thinking in new ways so the absolute uniqueness of who I am finds its way into art I can share with others. It's about teaching others that they can play…and out of that play can come the art that no one else could ever have made. I firmly believe that in each of us is a wellspring of creativity.

Today, altered book artists are exploring the possibilities of working with both the book's content and with the book itself as a physical object. They delight in transforming existing images and text into something entirely new. Most observers trace altered book art's current popularity back to the mid-1960s when British artist Tom Phillips began using the pages of an obscure Victorian novel, W. H. Mallock's *A Human Document*, as the canvas for his reinvention of the original work. The result, *A Humument*, was first privately published in 1970. Intending to eventually alter every page of the original novel, Phillips continues working on this project to this day, with new editions of *A Humument* appearing periodically. Inspired by his work, artists are continually finding new ways to cover, cut, and change books. They turn them into anything from shrines to colorful images that have little or nothing to do with the books they started out as.

What I want everyone to know about altering books is that it's a great platform for thinking creatively. When I create art by altering books, I find I can explore and express my unique creativity. I fashion art that's mine and mine alone…art that looks like no one else's art. We can all do that. Mostly, I think we just have to be inspired to ask the right question…for me, that question is "What if?"

TOM PHILLIPS, *A Humument*, page 8. Photo courtesy of Artists Rights Society New York/DACS, London

What if? That's what *New Directions in Altered Books* is all about.

FROM THEN TO NOW

When embarking on an adventure, I think it always helps to understand how that adventure is rooted in our shared human experience. When it comes to altered books, we need to travel all the way back to prehistoric times.

If you think of books broadly, if you see them as a way for one person to communicate with another when they don't happen to be in the same room, then you can certainly think of rock paintings and carvings as an early form of the book. And it turns out that right from the very beginning, our ancestors altered even these pictographs and petroglyphs. In the caves of France, Spain, and North America, we can see where an artist drew over earlier cave paintings…sometimes adding to them, at other times creating whole new visual messages out of older, faded sections.

Photo courtesy of Jim Zintgraff

We know the ancient Sumerians had invented cuneiform writing and were keeping records by about 3000 BC. They pressed characters into clay and left the tablets to dry in the sun. As a book alterer, I have to wonder, "Did they ever re-wet

Photo courtesy of the Cuneiform Digital Library Initiative, University of California at Los Angeles and the Max Planck Institute for the History of Science

those tablets, smooth them some, and then write on them anew?"

By the 11th century, the practice of altering books had veered off in another direction. Medieval Italian monks recycled old manuscripts, a practice that reminds us of just how precious and valuable books were at the time. This painstaking process involved scraping ink off the surface of delicate vellum pages. The monks were then able to place new texts and illustrations on top of the old, resulting in a palimpsest, or a manuscript where the old text still shows through.

In the late 19th century, Victorians amused themselves by illustrating books with engravings torn from other books, a practice known as Grangerism. In effect, they used the old books as scrapbooks, filling their pages with pasted ephemera, such as magazine images, personal recipes, and family pictures.

Not all book altering involves changing a volume's structure or ornamenting its pages. For example, readers who draw sketches or make comments or notations in page margins, called marginalia, are practicing a simple form of book altering. In this vein, New York artist Nancy Chunn, altered every

NANCY CHUNN, *Front Pages*, 1996
Courtesy of Ronald Feldman Fine Arts, New York

So when you alter a book, you're part of a very long tradition that is deeply embedded in what it means to be human. You're expressing a basic human drive to use symbols—from cuneiform to words to images—to communicate with others, often superimposing your thoughts and perceptions on top of what has gone before.

A WHOLE NEW PALETTE

That thousands of us alter books today is due in large part to Johannes Guttenberg, the 15th-century inventor of the modern printing press. Guttenberg's invention meant that books were no longer the precious, valuable items they once were. In fact, today they've become so commonplace that we recycle them into paper towels and toilet paper—and then dump them into our landfills. As a result, we now find ourselves in a different dilemma: instead of too few books, we might in fact have too many. Rather than seeing old books as a waste product, how much more respectful it is for us to turn them into art!

But suggesting a more respectful way of disposing of old books is only one small part of my motivation for writing this book. What I want to do with *Mixed-Media Books* is to step outside the kinds of mainstream, commercial expressions that tend to make my art look like yours. Already there are several published works on altering books. Many of them are excellent, but the focus tends to be on ways to decorate pages. With this book, I want to hand you a whole palette of colors. If you're currently in the habit of painting only in blue, I want to offer you not only new colors but also a whole new approach to paint; I want to say, "Mix up some brand new colors we've never seen. Excite us all!"

So, yes, this book has projects between its covers, 15 of them all told. But if you're like me, you already know that because the first thing you did was to check out the project section. In Testing the Tried and True, there are projects that ask the question, "What if an altered book were art and

New York Times front page in 1996, with her visually satirical additions. Then there were the artists of the late 19th and early 20th centuries who incorporated parts of books into their art. For example, artists such as Pablo Picasso and Georges Braque, as well as the Surrealists, collaged printed matter into their work.

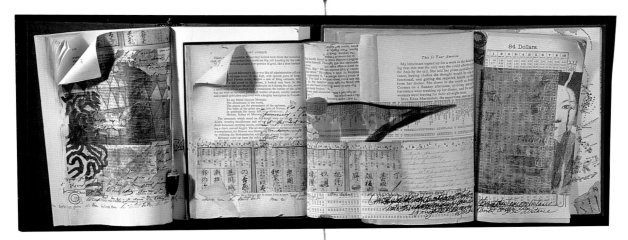

DEBRA DRESLER
Bridging the Distance, 2004
Antique book, original photographs, found objects
This sculptural work is attached to a backboard and wired to
hang on the wall.

functional at the same time?" In To Boldly Go, I've
included projects that challenge you to re-think
what an altered book can be. I'd love to inspire you
with these projects to find new ways to draw on
your life experiences and to use all kinds of art
processes so that what results is nothing short of
revolutionary altered book art. I hope you don't
construct exact duplicates of my projects; I think of
that approach as "follow the leader art."
Duplicating a project can be important if it teaches
us skills that send us down a new creative path.
The danger is we can get stuck if we don't follow
that creative path out the door into new territory.

You can figure it all out yourself… make it up.
Your creativity has very little to do with which glue,
tool, or paint you use. Your creativity depends on
how well you listen to your wise internal self…and
then whether you can summon the courage to pur-
sue what you hear. So do try these projects…but as
you do, always ask yourself, "What else could I
think of doing with this?" In the short Springboard
pieces scattered throughout the book, I make some
suggestions to help you answer that question.

While I certainly do see creating altered books as a
way of reaching inside, of listening to the deepest

parts of myself, and then creating work that
expresses my uniqueness, that is not to say that I
fool myself into thinking I create my altered books
in a vacuum. So in Crossover Artists, I feature the
thoughts and works of 12 artists who have come to
the altered book art from other disciplines—from
writing and photography to ceramics and environmental art. And in A Common Enterprise: The Art
of Working with Others, I describe how bands of
artists, from local groups to online communities to
institutions, are exploring new ways of collaborat-
ing with each other to create altered books. I also
include a discussion of successful approaches to
working with kids.

The gallery section features the altered book work
of others who are showing us inventive ways to
think about altering books: subversives all, they
entice us out of the art box, the box where our art
looks alike. They shine a light on just how many
other possibilities for altered books there are. They
are pioneers who invite you to create the art that
only you can make.

My final wish…I hope that someone alters this
book, too (well, as long as it isn't yours on loan).
Wouldn't that be the best?

GETTING STARTED

What are the basic rules that apply to altering books? There are no rules, and that's how is should be. In the world of altered books, you're more than welcome to just artfully tear pages out of an old book…no tools or techniques required.

However, while there may not be any hard and fast rules, I do talk about some basic methods in this chapter. That's because, as with any art form, there are some ways of creating altered books that are easier, more artful, and make more sense than other methods. I also offer a few design principles; understanding these principles can increase your chances of coming out at the other end of your project feeling that it's been a success.

What I don't discuss here are decorating techniques.

There are plenty of very good books out there with this information already. This book focuses on new ways of turning books into art, including using structural techniques, as well as some new decorative ideas, such as using no decoration at all.

What I want to do in this book is encourage you to tap into your own creative source. So when it comes to decorating any part of your project, I say, "Go make it up, or have an 'art accident'… or, even better, invent a completely new way to solve the problem."

CHOOSING THE RIGHT BOOK

THE BOOKS WE USE IN ALTERED BOOK ART ARE usually of the mass-produced, hardcover, or board book varieties. How you intend to alter the book determines the specific type of book you'll choose. The first general guideline (I almost wrote rule) is don't use a book that is precious to you or to anyone else in your family until you've mastered the necessary techniques. So you should probably wait to use the old family *Bible* or a favorite childhood storybook—if you alter them at all—until you're sure of exactly why you want to alter them and how to go about it.

You should also think carefully about what you require in terms of a book's weight and general condition. For example, if you're going to seal the book closed and cut a niche (see Cutting a Niche on page 31), then the type or condition of the book doesn't really matter; any reasonably thick book will do. However, if you're going to hang your book on the wall or if it's going to lie open, then a smaller, lighter book is a better choice.

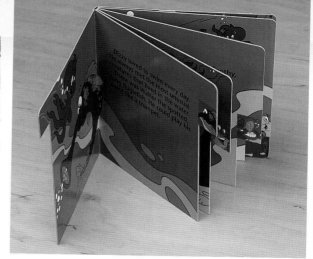

PHOTO 1

For the projects in this book, you'll generally work with three types of books: board, sewn signature, and perfect bound books. Knowing the pros and cons of the different binding styles is important.

BOARD BOOKS

The main difference between board books and sewn signature, or perfect bound, books is that board books have pages made of heavy, plastic-coated chipboard paper. After gluing the pages to each other into a block, printers then attach the block directly to the front and back covers, leaving the area over the spine free and eliminating the need for endpapers.

This is Your Book...

Books...We see them everywhere: in libraries and classrooms, occasionally forgotten and left on a park bench, maybe even being carried around in your dog's mouth.

When you open up your book, you'll find its pages, collectively called the *text block*. Look at two facing pages (called a *spread*), and take note of the *gutter*, or the junction of two sheets of the text block. (It's the spot where you often tuck your bookmark.)

Usually a book's pages aren't printed one by one but in multiples of four on large sheets of paper called *signatures*; each page is carefully placed so that when the signature is folded after printing and trimmed down to the final page size, the pages appear in the right order. Printers use adhesives, thread, and various other methods to attach the signatures to each other to form the *binding*. Whatever the binding method used, the text block in most books is attached to the covers with *endpapers*, sheets of

strong, heavy paper. One side of the endpaper is glued to the inside cover; the other is attached to the text block's outermost page.

Examining the outside of the book, we find the covers and the *spine*. The front and back covers are usually made of a hard paperboard, called *bookboard*, which is often covered with decorative paper or fabric. Connecting the front and back covers and located over the binding is the *spine* (figure 1).

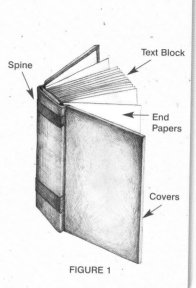

FIGURE 1

Binding and Spine Stress

In the process of adding elements to a book, you can produce so much stress on its spine and binding that the spine breaks and pages begin to fall out. The main culprits are 3-D embellishments and certain types of niches.

When you close a book over a 3-D embellishment, the extra bulk will cause the binding and the spine to stretch. The bigger, harder, and closer to the spine the embellishment, the more stress it causes and the faster the binding deteriorates.

Cutting a niche can have the same effect. Normally, the edge of each page of an open book falls just short of the edge of the page beneath it. This protects the spine by dissipating

the pressure the pages exert. As you'll discover in Cutting a Niche on page 31, when you construct a niche, you glue a block of pages together. That, of course, forces the pages to act as a unit. So every time you open the book, you'll stress the binding by pulling the entire block of pages away from the spine edge of the book. You'll place the greatest stress on the binding if you create a page block for a niche in the middle of the book.

Because they're among the sturdiest of books, board books are a good choice for those first altered book projects (photo 1 on page 11). The only drawback is that board books are plastic-coated, so they require a little more preparation than other books (see Preparing Your Book on page 14), but the preparation work is easy.

SEWN SIGNATURE BOOKS

Printers once commonly formed the text block by sewing the individual signatures to each other and then gluing them together, using a special cloth and

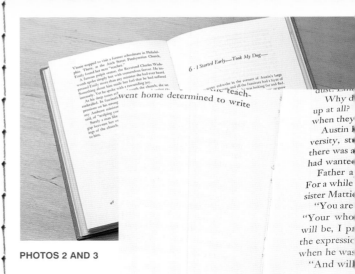

PHOTOS 2 AND 3

paper (photo 2). You'll be able to tell it's a sewn signature book because if you look closely, you'll detect stitches in the center of each signature (photo 3).

There are a number of advantages to seeking out these older books. In general, sewn signature pages stand up better to altering than do those in newer books. In particular, the sewn signature's sturdier binding is less prone to binding and spine stress. However, you'll need to look through a sewn signature book carefully. You'll often find that the acid-based paper used is deteriorating or crumbling. And as the books age, the pages show foxing, or dark rust-colored or brown spots. The biggest disadvantage to sewn signature books is they're getting hard-

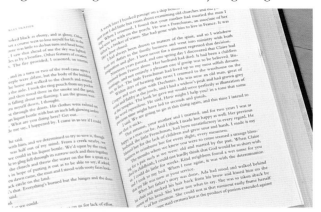

PHOTO 4

er to find, as most modern publishers employ cheaper, less time-consuming methods, such as perfect binding discussed below.

If you've decided that a sewn signature book is the best choice for your project, look for them in old boxes, on your aunt's dusty shelves, or at garage and estate sales. One of the best places to search for sewn signature books is at library sales. The books found there are generally in good shape and dirt cheap, plus the monies go right back into buying new books for your community.

PERFECT BOUND BOOKS

More common today than sewn signature books are perfect bound books (photo 4). In these books, the printer forms text blocks first by clamping and then by gluing the signatures together. In some cases, the signatures are also glued to the spine. As you search through the book, you won't find any evidence of stitching in the center of the individual signatures.

Perfect bound books are plentiful and easy to find. And you're more likely to find heavier weight paper as well as glossy art and photographs in perfect bound books. However, both the sewn signature and the board book will hold up better to altering than the perfect bound book in almost all cases. In particular, it's much easier to create binding and spine stress in perfect bound books than it is in sewn signature books, and that makes it especially difficult to add 3-D embellishments and have the book stay intact.

CLAUDIA M. MORALES
Let Go, 2004
Gesso, graphite, charcoal, acrylic paint, collage map, dictionary paper, stencils, lotteria cards
Pages appear in Jill Valle's California collaborative book

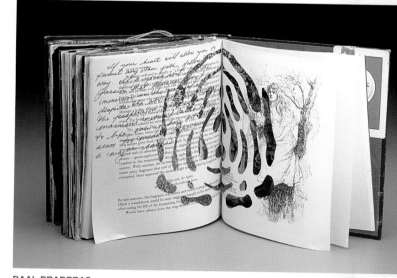

DAAL PRADERAS
Layers, 2004
Abstract stencil created from Spanish soap box flowers
Pages appear in Claudia Morales McCain's California collaborative book

PREPARING YOUR BOOK

AFTER YOU'VE CHOSEN THE BOOK YOU WANT TO alter, it's time to get the surfaces ready. The way you prepare a book depends on the type of book you've decided to use.

PREPARING BOARD BOOKS

Stamp inks, paints, and even some types of glue do not adhere well to a board book's plastic-coated pages. The solution is to prepare the surface in one of three ways—tearing off, sanding, or sealing the plastic layer (photo 5).

- **Tear off the plastic layer.** This is a low-tech solution many artists prefer because it doesn't require any tools or materials. What results is a textured, absorbent surface. The downside is it takes time and leaves a bumpy surface, which I personally find harder to work with.

- **Sand the plastic layer.** You need to sand just enough to create a "tooth," or dull surface. This method creates a smoother surface than the one produced by simply tearing off the plastic, but it also creates a messy, dusty residue (if you care about such things). The residue can pose a problem for someone with asthma.

- **Paint the book with a primer or sealer** used to cover plastic, glass, or metal surfaces. You can buy an easy-to-clean-up, water-based sealer at any hardware store. While using a primer or sealer will give you a surface you can work on, the disadvantage is that this method takes time: You need to apply the primer or sealer in sections to ensure that that pages don't stick together, and then allow time for each section to dry overnight. Gesso will not permanently bond to the plastic unless the plastic has been sanded first.

PREPARING SEWN SIGNATURE AND PERFECT BOUND BOOKS

If you're going to alter a sewn signature or perfect bound book that people can page through, I recommend you prepare the book by following these procedures.

- Glue two or three pages together to create a sturdier surface on which to work (photo 6). This is particularly necessary if your book has thin, lightweight pages. It's usually best to strengthen your pages first and then decorate. Generally, any favorite glue will work when you're attaching

PHOTO 5   Sanded   Sealed with primer   Plastic torn away

PHOTO 6

the pages to each other. However, if for any reason you want to decorate your pages first or if you want to cover the back side of a decorated page, a sheet adhesive can be a good choice because it bonds instantly and smoothly.

• Remove a minimum of twice as many pages as you leave in the book to compensate for the thickness of the materials you're adding. This is necessary because whenever you're adding paints, papers, or any other item, you're adding bulk. Remove the pages by cutting or tearing them at least ¼ inch from the gutter (photo 7). Eliminating pages won't allow the altered book to close neatly; it'll never do that. But it will reduce the stress on the binding. (see Binding and Spine Stress, page 12).

• You'll need to remove even more pages than suggested above if you're adding particularly thick items. For example, you'd need to take out at least five pages to make room for one bingo card or for a piece of flocked ribbon.

PHOTO 7

KIM GRANT
Home and Wings, 2004
Altered book; acrylics, inkjet transfers, photocopies, photos, copper tape, studs, gold leaf

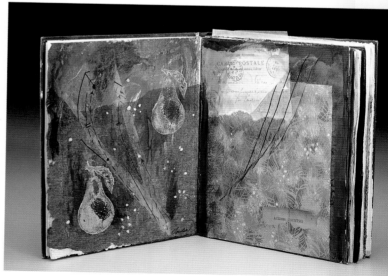

CLAUDIA M. MORALES
Appears in Rebecca Caro's California collaborative book

DESIGN PRINCIPLES

You've chosen and prepared your book. Now it's time to plan exactly how you're going to alter it. Sometimes, you'll look at a piece of altered book art and say, "Wow!" I suspect your response is related to two things: The project is well-designed, and it's innovative. It's like nothing you've ever seen before, and perhaps like nothing you've ever thought of yourself. There are a lot of elements that make up a good design. We can't cover them all here, but I will talk about symmetrical and asymmetrical designs as well as the importance of proportion and continuity.

SYMMETRY VS. ASYMMETRY

You probably intuitively know a lot about symmetry and asymmetry. Symmetry is simply an arrangement in which the elements to the left and those to the right of a central point are mirror repetitions of each other (photo 8). It looks like this: MXI o IXM. On the other hand, while there is certainly a sense of balance in asymmetry, all of the elements are unique. So an asymmetrical design will look something like this: Pido x alyg (photo 9).

Your choice of a symmetrical or asymmetrical design has important implications for your composition. The more symmetrical your composition, the less energy it has. This is true even if you've arranged a large number of identical, mirrored elements around a central point that contains an odd surprise. That's because once you've taken in the design, your eye feels as if its work is mostly done. A symmetrical design is a good choice for those times you want your art to convey a sense of safety and repose.

In contrast (photo 9), a well-balanced, asymmetrical composition invites the eye to move among its elements, spurred on by the urge to relate them to each other. It is a more energetic design that demands that the viewer interact with it in a way that a static symmetrical design doesn't.

PHOTO 8

PHOTO 9

PROPORTION

How do you achieve a balanced asymmetrical design? You need to be mindful of proportion, or the harmonious relationship of parts to each other and to the whole. For the ancient Greeks, proportion was an important attribute of beauty. The Greek mathematician Euclid first calculated what has come to be known as the Golden Proportion or the Golden Ratio: roughly 3 to 5. It's widely believed the

PHOTO 10
Above, and to the left
JODY ALEXANDER,
Max and The Filipino Twins, 2004
Calligraphic writing in pen and ink, Coptic binding, encaustic paint, artificial sinew; pages rebound

Greeks felt this was the ideal proportion and used it as an important design principle for their art and architecture. What all this means for us as we plan our altered books is that we should aim for a well-balanced asymmetry (photo 10). Also we should keep in mind that a proportion on the order of 3 to 5 often results in a particularly pleasing design.

What kinds of elements are we trying to balance? We're trying to strike a balance among different colors, textures, and shapes, light and dark, whether images are related or not, and the various other properties of an object. Just keep in mind that the more you have going on in your art, the more difficult it is to maintain that pleasing balance. If you change one element, it can affect relationships along several continuums. For example, add a shiny, round, hard, red bottle cap to your altered book, and see what happens. Instantly, you've changed the relationships among the various colors and shapes and shifted the balance between hard and soft as well as shiny and dull objects.

This all gives a whole new meaning to the art principle, "Less is more." While I'm not arguing for keeping your art simple, I am advocating that when you design and embellish your altered book, you always think about balance and proportion. Ask yourself, "So, does my composition really need that next thing I was going to glue onto the page?"

CHECKING IT ALL OUT

Put your piece of art in front of you for a final look. Close your eyes. Now open them, and note what catches your eye first. Then where does your eye move next? And does it move naturally, or have you moved on because you've wearied of looking at the first thing? Does your eye ever get bored and wander off the page entirely?

Ideally, the first thing that should catch your attention is the composition's focal point, the element you've designed to be its main point of interest. Then, your eye should work its way through the entire piece, led on over bridges formed by color and line (both actual and inferred) to the next area, until it has seen it all. At no point should your eye leave the page so that you have to start your examination all over again. Photos 11 and 12 are good examples of well-balanced composition and focal point.

Turn your composition sideways in both directions and then upside down; the piece should work no matter which way you turn it, as is true of the photo to the right. Each time, look at it with fresh eyes. If your eye gets stuck in one spot or jumps off the page, consider making some bridges between elements or removing ones that impede the flow. Remember: it's never too late to listen closely to your creative instincts and make changes.

Continuity

Most artists I know have some version of an idea diary. In it go things that might contain the seeds of some future piece of artwork: a sketch, a short note to ourselves, quotes, a laying down of colors side by side that we might want to try together, textile swatches, actual pictures of another artist's work that inspires us. Artist's idea books are creative. They are not art.

What distinguishes all good art that I have ever seen is that it has cohesion…continuity…all of its parts contribute to the whole. And the "whole" that results from all those parts is a whole new entity. An artist has acted creatively on various materials and produced something else entirely…a work of art.

While Rande Hanson's book *Galeríe del la Danse* and McNall Mason's book *My Life as a Paper Bag* both started as board books, they're very different in style. Rande's book on dance is filled with simple words and rich colors. Each page relates to the one before and the one after,

and there is a flow to the book's theme and style. McNall's book is word-rich…an original story. The style of its art is both consistent and so complex that it takes viewers several readings before they can find all the visual references and surprises. Despite the differences in their styles, both Rande and McNall are dead-on when it comes to achieving continuity and cohesion. Both Rande and McNall's books hold together as solid works of altered book art.

RANDE HANSON
Galeríe de la Danse, 2003
Collage, magazine pictures,
acrylic paint, rubber stamps

MCNALL MASON
My Life as a Bag, 2003
Board book; tipped-in pages

TOOLS AND MATERIALS

Suggesting which tools and materials to gather for your altered book projects will influence the types of altering you do. It's unavoidable. So because I want this book to be about how we can discover our unique creative selves through altering books, I really want you to hear something I have to say. *You can create great altered books with no special tools or art materials at all.*

Having made that clear, here are some tools and materials I often find myself using…as well as some alternatives I've discovered.

CUTTING TOOLS

When you don't have the right tool handy, you'll find that your mind will flip into the "other possibility" mode. You may surprise yourself with the alternatives you come up with. Still, if you have a vision for a project that includes cutting a niche or a window in a book cover, you'll need a sharp knife—or you'll have to revise your plans.

KNIVES. Craft knives, snap-blade disposables, and utility knives are the three types of knives you'll use most often when doing altered book art. The light-est duty, most precise knife is the craft knife with its pencil-shaped handle. Because you can obtain interchangeable blades for these knives, you're always guaranteed both a sharp blade, which is especially important when you're trying to make a clean cut in paper, and a variety of blade types that are suitable for different materials and situations.

The snap-blade disposable is an inexpensive, medium-duty knife that comes in a variety of weights. It's easy to keep sharp: you simply snap off a section as it becomes dull. Because you can extend this knife's blade, it's handy for those times you need to make a deeper cut into your book. Just make sure you're very careful when cutting with a fully extended snap blade. It's flexible, so it breaks off easily.

The most heavy-duty knife is the utility knife. Although it has replaceable blades like the craft knife, replacing them is a little more complicated. This is the best knife to use if you are cutting a window into a book cover (see Cutting Windows and Doors, page 29). However, if you're cutting a cover into pieces and you feel comfortable using power tools, a band saw or a jigsaw is a good labor-saving device.

Assorted cutting tools. From left, craft knife, snap-blade knife, utility knife, zigzag scissors, deckle scissors

OTHER GREAT TOOLS. You'll often find yourself using all kinds of scissors, both plain ones and any of the many varieties of specialty scissors (such as deckle or zigzag) that you can use to create interesting edges and effects. A good paper cutter is useful as well.

ALTERNATIVES. You can tear things out by hand or use a single-edged razor blade. Don't experiment with kitchen knives or pocket knives, though, especially ones with dull blades. You could hurt yourself.

JODY ALEXANDER
Chimed Awful, 2004
Altered book; encaustic paint, beeswax, found objects

APPLICATION TOOLS

We often find ourselves applying glues and colors, rubbing plant materials or dirt on pages, or spraying them with aerosols. What we're applying to a surface does influence what application tool might be best for the job.

GREAT TOOLS. It's good to have brushes (both bristle and foam), craft sticks, toothpicks, sponges, and rags on hand.

ALTERNATIVES TO USING TOOLS. Using my fingers is my tried and true favorite technique for applying all kinds of things—or how about trying droppers, sticks, or cotton swabs? You'll also find that an expired credit card can function as a great squeegee when you're removing excess paint from papers and fabrics.

PROTECTIVE TOOLS

You'll find you need to protect all kinds of things when you're doing altered book projects. You'll want to shield one section of your book while you're working on another, prevent damage to your work space, and protect yourself from potentially toxic materials.

GREAT TOOLS. Self-healing cutting mats are frequently useful. They range in size from that of a small book to a 36-inch tabletop version. You can use these mats both to protect your work surface and to prevent you from cutting too deeply into a book. Inserting release papers into your book will keep the masked areas safe from accidentally applying paint and glue. Protect your hands from chemical toxins with nitrile gloves and your lungs from dust or vapors by wearing a face mask.

Protective tools. Self-healing cutting mat, gloves, plastic wrap, waxed paper, release paper

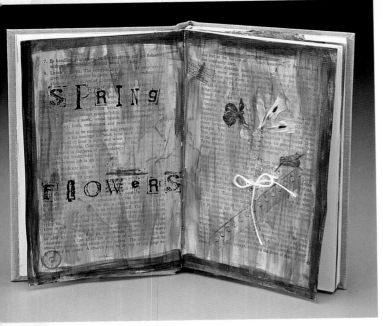

JONNA BARNETT
Two spreads from *Spring Flowers*, 2005
Recycled products, springs from ball point pens, dried flowers, wine
bottle seal, papers, stamps, acrylic paint, glazes

ALTERNATIVES. There are all kinds of cheap alternatives to purchased protective tools. For example, you can use waxed paper or plastic wrap instead of release papers. And it's never a bad idea to do any work that generates dust and toxic vapors outside.

OTHER TOOLS

A bone folder comes in handy when burnishing an area you've glued, or sharpening a fold. The relatively inexpensive plastic version will work just fine. You can also use a table knife handle or any smooth, straight object you can easily hold in your hand.

A metal ruler with a cork back is a multipurpose tool. It stays put. It both measures and can serve as a marking and a cutting guide. While any ruler will work if you're marking and measuring, a metal edge is essential if you want to use it as a cutting guide.

Then there are hole punches, a pencil sharpener, a sketchbook to hold your ideas and lists of things you want to try, your computer with its printer and scanner, a digital camera, drills, a band saw…It is all good, and none of it is absolutely necessary.

ATTACHMENT MATERIALS

ADHESIVES. "What kind of glue should I use?" That's the most frequently asked question among newcomers to book altering. I find there is never a consensus as to which glue is best.

There is no substitute for trying different glues yourself and recording the results. I recommend having an old book you use just for testing glues and experimenting with techniques. To see what works best under different circumstances, use different glues and attach a wide variety of decorations and objects into your practice book. I still have mine from years ago. I glued pages together with different glues and made notes directly on the page about what glue I'd used and how I'd applied it.

Table 1 summarizes the key information about the most common adhesives.

Table 1. Most Commonly Used Adhesives

Type	Application	Advantages	Disadvantages	Best use	Remedies
Glue Stick	Rubs on.	Not messy; very portable.		Paper to paper.	
White Craft Glue	Apply thinly with foam brush, fingers, or a credit card edge.	Different formulations for just about any purpose.	Liquid; dries reasonably clear (though it isn't as clear as glass).	Multiuse, depending on formulation.	
Pastes	Apply thinly with credit card.	Stays put; doesn't wick into other areas.	Takes forever to dry if applied too liberally; thick application can produce molding and discoloration.	Paper to paper.	No cure for molding.
Sheet Adhesive (film only)	Basically very wide, double-stick tape; lay material to be glued onto the sheet adhesive and cut off excess; remove backing and attach the item to the surface you're gluing it to.	Bonds instantly; great for bonding irregular surfaces together; e.g., attaching fabric to an uneven surface.	Bonds instantly on contact; leaves some adhesive behind on cutting implements.	Any type of lightweight surfaces, such as fabric, paper, book board, etc.	Clean scissors with nail polish remover.
Sheet Adhesive (with stabilizer)	Same as above.	Doesn't bond until pressure is applied; allows some open time to reposition if surfaces not pressed firmly together.	Residue sticks to cutting implements; only works on smooth surfaces.	Bonds dissimilar surfaces, such as metal to wood, paper to smooth stone, etc.	Clean scissors and knives with nail polish remover.
Sticker Machine	Feed paper item through a machine.	Creates stickers by applying film directly to the back of paper.	Film extends slightly beyond edge of sticker.	Good for quick, easy bonding of small pieces of paper.	Clean film from edges with nail polish remover.
Acrylic Medium	Apply liquid matte varieties with foam brush; apply thicker gels with fingers or a craft stick.	Bonds both porous and nonporous surfaces together, regardless of texture; offers a long open time to reposition; can be tinted with acrylic paint.	Longer drying time; cures to a solid in two hours, but complete curing takes 24 hours.	Bonds any surface, including plastic; great for gluing paper to paper or bonding page edges into a block; gel particularly good for 3-D attachments; gloss dries the clearest.	Plan other activities while the glue dries.
Fusible Web	Cut section just larger than item to be bonded; apply web to back of item, and iron on; trim off excess; remove paper backing, and iron onto other surface.	Instant bonding; leaves no residue.	Only works on unpainted, flat surfaces (so the iron can apply heat evenly).	Flat bond for paper and fabric that has nothing on it that can be harmed by the iron's heat; webbing sticks to the iron if wrong side accidentally ironed.	Pay close attention to which side you are ironing, or get a nonstick cover for your iron that you can use while working with fusible web.
Bead and Glass Silicone Glue	Use an implement such as a toothpick or craft stick to spread glue.	Bonds uneven and dissimilar surfaces permanently; retains flexibility.	Solvent-based glue with unpleasant odor.	3-D and nonabsorbent surfaces.	Requires adequate ventilation.
Contact Cement	Apply thinly to both surfaces; allow to dry.	Indestructible and permanent bond for hard or dense surfaces.	Impossible to reposition once surfaces touch each other.	Good coverage over large surfaces, such as gluing wood or leather onto covers.	Insert paper between surfaces to prevent premature contacts; gradually remove paper to bond.

OTHER ATTACHMENT MATERIALS. Don't limit yourself to adhesives when you need to attach one thing to another. Other options include eyelets, brads, staples, rivets, various kinds of tape, paper clips...or make holes you can use to sew or string substances like wire, ribbons, or yarns. Even paint works as an attachment material if you apply something to it while wet.

COLORING MATERIALS

GESSO. Gesso isn't strictly intended for use as a colorant, but color it does. In fact, it comes in many different colors, including clear. Because it prepares a surface to "grab" onto other colorants and adhesives, I'm including it here.

OTHER COLORING MATERIALS. Paints, stamping inks, and colored pens and pencils are the most obvious colorants. Other options fill the shelves of craft, art, office supply, and hardware stores, but anything that leaches or causes color, like old tea bags, burnt plant materials...you can experiment with all of these.

Assorted decorative papers, fibers, and coloring tools

GIGI STARNES
An Altered Adventure: Torn Plaid, 2004
Gesso, acrylic, watercolor, gauze, fabric softener, CD, compass, decorative punches, rubber stamps, dried leaves, ribbon, magazine pictures, felt-tipped pens

PAPERS, FIBERS, AND FABRICS

You can use paper and fabric both as structural material (e.g., fold-outs, tip-ins, pockets, and hinges) and for decoration. When you're using such materials as structural elements, it's handy to have different weights from which to choose. Think of sturdy watercolor papers, Tyvek, heavy cardstocks as well as thin tissues and translucent vellum.

When decorating our books, we can include words and pictures culled from other books and magazines, printouts from our computer, handmade papers, our own photographs, commercial decorative papers, junk mail, and other found paper. And that's just the paper possibilities. Yarns, fabrics, ribbons, and other things made from fabric can be fun to work with; you can not only decorate with them, but you can also use them to make hinges and other attachment devices.

EMMA POWELL
Trapped, 2000
Salvaged book, beach detritus

I always use as much rejectamenta (recycled materials) as possible in my work. As this recycled book was about fishing, there were a lot of visual references to nets and grids; I used this as my starting point. Once I had located the word "trapped" in the text, this became the main theme and text and images were trapped in various ways throughout the book.

3-D FINDS

To find great objects that you can use in your altered book project, you really only have to remind yourself to notice things as you walk through your life. Although you'll occasionally come across a terrific 3-D find at a thrift shop, generally you don't need to purchase such items. Old hardware, broken bits you pick up on a walk…game pieces, broken jewelry, pieces of wood left over from a building project, dead paint brushes, old toys…The adventure of finding these in unexpected places never ends, so remember to use what you pick up—and the sooner the better, so they don't get lost in a pile.

Decorating Arsenal

Decorating arsenal: this is a code word for the materials you'll use to "art-ify" your altered book creations. Your arsenal could simply consist of glue, gesso, a sponge you use to apply it, and a pencil. Most of us, though, fill our creative spaces with things like paints, brushes, ink pads, stamps we buy or carve, adhesives, decorative papers, glossy magazines, found objects, fibers…a never-ending list that just keeps growing as we explore new techniques.

Your altered book arsenal will not be a static collection of materials and tools, but one that changes as you try out new art materials or see a new way to use an art material that has been gathering dust for a while. And it doesn't need to actually be a conventional art product. Differently colored soils, used tea bags, junk mail…it's all good for making altered books.

PHOTO 14
NORIHO URIU, 2004
Printed on vellum
Tipped-in pages appear in Jill Valle's California collaborative book

TECHNIQUES FOR ALTERING BOOKS

In this book, I make it a practice to encourage you to decide how you want to decorate a project. What follows are not only book altering techniques specified in project instructions but also some other basic methods that might inspire you as you're contemplating exactly how to make a project reflect your own personal style and taste.

ADDING SIMPLE ELEMENTS

Sometimes the simplest techniques are the best. You can insert tip-ins, fold-outs, and all sorts of 3-D objects into the book you're altering.

TIP-INS. For centuries, people have been using tip-ins as a way of adding engravings or protecting art. They are new pages or vellum overlays added to a book (photos 13 and 14). You can use the traditional method of attaching tip-ins by applying a thin bead of glue to the edge of the sheet to be bound into the book and then inserting it wherever you want—in the gutter, for instance, or along the top edge of a page (photo 15).

PHOTO 15
MCNALL MASON
My Life as a Bag, 2003
Board book; tipped-in pages

You can also use a hinge to attach a tip-in (photo 16). Cut paper or fabric to the length of the sheet you're going to fasten to the book page and fold the strip in half. Glue half to either the top or the underside of the new page and the other half to the book. If you make your hinges out of decorative paper or fabric, they will be decorative as well as functional.

PHOTO 16

FOLD-OUTS. A fold-out is simply a hinged page you add to your book's cover or to any of its pages (photos 17 and 18). It needs to be stronger than a tip-in because it has to stay attached to the book despite repeated folding and unfolding (photo 19).

When designing a fold-out page, remember it needs to be slightly narrower than the rest of the book's pages or it won't fit inside when folded closed (photo 20, as shown on page 28). Make it out of sturdy, heavyweight paper, such as cardstock, watercolor, pastel, or cover-weight papers or out of a couple of pages you've glued together. The strip you use to hinge a fold-out must be strong, flexible, lightweight, and hold a crease. Watercolor paper, cover-weight paper, Tyvek, book cloth, or closely woven cotton are good choices for this type of hinge.

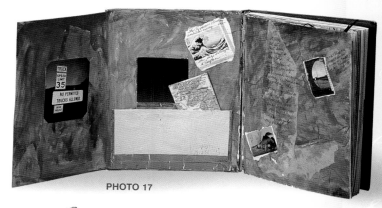

PHOTO 17

PHOTO 19

Top and bottom:
GABE CYR
Age of Exploration
Pages shown illustrate fold-outs

PHOTO 18
DAAL PRADERAS
Smog Centerfold, 2004
Fold-out page appears in Beth Parson's
California collaborative book

To attach the fold-out, simply butt the new page against the page to which you're attaching it and cover the joint with the hinge (photos 21 and 22). When the adhesive dries, turn the page over and apply a second hinge strip to the other side (photo 23). Allow the adhesive to dry before closing the fold-out page completely.

3-D EMBELLISHMENT. You can add all kinds of 3-D embellishments to your altered book. Just remember that you want to avoid gluing 3-D objects close to the spine because they're likely to cause binding and spine stress (see Binding and Spine Stress, page 12). Also, you'll need to remove enough pages to compensate for the thickness of the objects you're adding.

Of course, a drawback to 3-D embellishments, no matter where you put them, is they create an uneven surface when you try to alter the other pages. You can avoid the problem by simply not using 3-D objects on your book pages. But there are several other solutions to try.

You can wait until the very end before adding such objects. If that's impractical, add the objects only to the outside edges. First glue several pages together to strengthen them, and then punch a hole ¼ inch from any edge; reinforce it with eyelets or heavy paper. You can then proceed to attach objects to the pages with ribbons, string, or yarn strung through the holes. That way, your objects will hang outside the book. Another way to avoid placing objects on the pages is by inserting them into an opening you've cut in your book. Such openings are called niches (see Cutting a Niche, page 31).

PHOTO 20

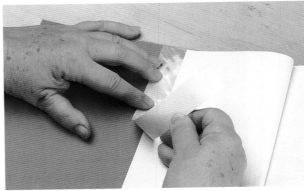
PHOTO 21 AND PHOTO 22

PHOTO 23

REMOVING A TEXT BLOCK

Sometimes, for example in the Sacred Spaces project (page 42), you'll want to use just the book covers. In other cases, such as Bend Me, Shape Me (page 57), it's the text block you'll require. In both instances, you'll need to detach the text block from the book covers.

It's easy. Just lay your opened book on a flat surface. With one hand (the one you don't use to do the cutting), grab the entire text block. Gently pull up on the text block, and you'll create a space between the endpaper and the cover (photo 24). Use a craft knife to slice through the endpapers from top to bottom (photo 25). Repeat for the other side of the text block (photo 26). That's all you need to do.

CUTTING WINDOWS AND DOORS

In Picture This! (page 36) and Celebration (page 72), you have examples of projects where you'll need to cut a window. That simply means you'll make an opening in one page that reveals something that's on the next page; sometimes you might decide to cut a flap that opens like a door (photo 27). When cutting windows and doors, there are two issues to consider.

Safe Cutting

Always cut away from your body, especially when cutting into a hard material. Naturally, the harder the material you're cutting into, the more pressure you'll apply. The more pressure you apply, the greater the possibility the knife will slip.

Use a series of lighter strokes that go a little deeper each time rather than cutting with a single stroke. In addition to reducing the chances of hurting yourself because the knife has slipped, employing lighter strokes will make it less likely you'll make an inaccurate cut.

PHOTO 24

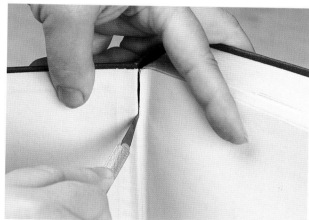

PHOTO 25

PHOTO 26

PHOTO 28
GABE CYR
Practice book illustrating focal elements that show through cut-out windows regardless of which way the window page is turned

The first one is the design consideration. If you've cut a complete opening in a page and that page turns, when you look through that opening, you should see a focal element, or the main point of interest, regardless of whether the opening is framing the page that comes before or after it (photos 28 and 29). In short, what shows through the opening has to make artistic sense. If you have a flap opening, attach a brad, string, or ribbon to serve as a door handle on both sides, so you can open it from either side. This is all common sense stuff, but it's sometimes easy to forget. If you keep these design considerations in mind, you'll have a piece of art that works both practically and aesthetically.

The second issue is how to cut the window or doors. First of all, unless you're working with a board book, it's easiest to decorate the page on which you're going to make the opening before you do any cutting. After deciding whether you want a complete opening or a flap, draw the shape on the page. Place a cutting mat or a piece of heavy cardboard underneath. For a window, use your metal-edged ruler as a

PHOTO 29

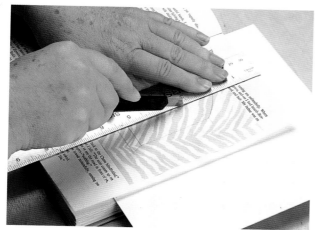

PHOTO 30

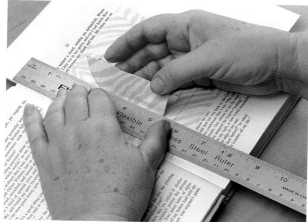

PHOTO 31

cutting guide by placing it against the lines you've drawn, and cut all sides of the opening with a craft knife (photo 30). For a door, simply leave the side that will act as the hinge uncut. To make sure your door hinge crease is sharp and straight, fold it against the ruler (photo 31). You can then attach whatever you've decided to use as a door handle.

CUTTING A NICHE

For many of these projects, you'll hollow out a part of your book. I can guarantee that you won't achieve a consistent result from one niche to the next. All kinds of things affect how a niche turns out: the humidity; the size and depth of the hole; and the

type, age, and condition of the paper, to name just a few factors. But that's not a problem. Basically, creating a niche is a three-stage process, which I describe and demonstrate on the next page.

CREATING A PAGE BLOCK

1. Isolate the pages that will form the page block with waxed or release paper; the paper will prevent you from accidentally gluing the block to an adjacent part of the book. You may want to use masking tape to secure the paper to the covers or to any pages that won't be a part of the text block.

Niche Basics

Here are some basic things to know about niches before you get started.

- Older books typically have more porous pages that resist clean cuts. This becomes even more of a problem in a humid environment…you'll feel as if you're trying to cut a wet cereal box, and the end result sometimes looks as if you'd chewed the page instead of cutting it. While this can create an interesting effect, if it's not what you want, choose a newer book, work in a less humid environment, or smooth out your niche with spackle or modeling paste once it's cut.

- If you plan to cut a deep niche, consider doing so in increments. Although you can extend the blade of a snap-blade disposable knife, it becomes unsteady when you do so.

- If you're going to have decorated pages as well as a niche in your book, consider decorating the pages first. It's best to have a flat, stable surface to work on when decorating. If the page you're decorating is resting on top of the niche hole, then you obviously no longer have a flat, stable surface. Also, it's best to decorate the page that serves as the background for the niche before you glue the niche to the adjoining parts of the book.

2. Next, use a foam brush to slather on glue (I like to use acrylic medium) or paint onto the page edges. Finally, clamp or weigh the page block down with heavy books until the glue dries. This will usually take anywhere from several hours to overnight. Remove the waxed or release paper once the block is dry.

CUTTING THE NICHE

1. Use a pencil to mark the shape of the niche on the top page of the block. Place the cutting mat or a piece of cardboard behind the back of the page block.

2. Use a knife with a fresh sharp blade, and cut along your lines. It'll be easier if you hold your knife against a metal-edged ruler for the first few layers (photo 32). Remove the pages as you cut them free. After you've cut a few pages down, you'll be using the edge of the previously cut section as your guide (photo 33). Continue until you've cut the niche to the desired depth.

3. If your cover will be part of a niche block, you can use the niche you've cut in the page block as a template. Trace its shape on the cover.

FINISHING THE NICHE

1. Re-insert the waxed or release paper between the niche and any adjacent part of the book, and apply glue, acrylic medium, or paint to the inside edges of the niche (photo 34). Clamp or weigh the book down again, and let dry.

2. Finally, wherever necessary you'll glue the niche to the adjoining parts of the book. Decorate any other parts of the niche, and if you wish, place items into the niche.

PHOTO 32

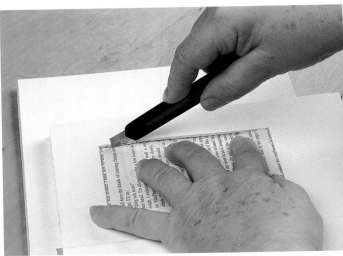

PHOTO 33

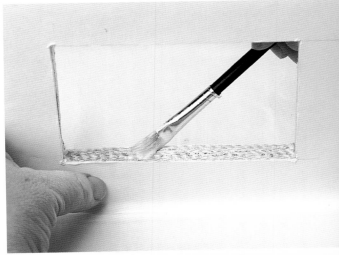

PHOTO 34

HANGERS

I confess that hanging mechanism techniques don't exactly qualify as basic techniques because most of the altered book community hasn't thought about hanging work yet. But when this happens, you'll be ahead of the pack.

The method you choose depends on the book's weight and whether you're going to hang it vertically or horizontally. Here are some ways to create hangers.

BRACE HANGER

If you're going to hang an opened book, like the Just Hanging Around project on page 52, you'll need to create a brace across the back of the book before you can attach the hanger to it. In addition to serving as a base for the hanging mechanism, the brace stabilizes the book and holds it open.

To do this, you'll first cut a strip from a book-cover remnant, lightweight cardboard, or piece of wood. Ideally, it will be about 3 inches tall and at least 1 inch narrower than the book. Next, you'll make three pencil lines on the wrong side (i.e., the side that doesn't show when attached to the book). Mark two spots that are 1 inch down from the top. Place a ruler so it touches both marks, and then draw a straight line across the strip's width. Now mark two more points, each point about 2 inches in from the side of the strip, and draw a short line through these points lengthwise. At each point where the lines intersect, use a craft knife to make two slits just long enough to accommodate either the brads or the eye screws from a picture hanging kit. Insert the brads or eye screws from the right side of the strip; if you're using brads, open the prongs. Center the strip on the back of the altered

Leaping Out of the Box

Creativity and creating art aren't the same thing…nor does someone necessarily have to "be an artist" to create art. Some of us spend our lives creating art. If we're not creating art, we don't feel alive. Others of us make art just once in a while, art that is a direct response to our creative urges.

It's fine to express our creative impulses by following leaders or trying something we've seen other folks do. This is often a great way to explore, to learn, and to gain confidence.

It's all good. But I think it's powerful to understand our creative selves and how we create art by acknowledging our uniqueness, our own personal way of making art.

Each of us processes our creative thought differently. At one end of the continuum are those of us who process our thoughts completely internally. We are more likely to be left-brain, linear thinkers. We fully plan what we're going to make before we begin and carefully plot out a sequence of steps that will help us arrive at our goals. At the other end are those of us who don't know what we're thinking until we express it in some tangible, external way. We just gather art materials and make up our art as we go along. Those of us who work this way are more likely to be right-brained, process-oriented thinkers. Most of us fall somewhere in between.

The point is just to know yourself and be aware. Watch yourself as you make art. What is it that feels natural? Know that when someone else shares his or her art and how he or she creates, it may or may not work for you. You have your own way that works best for you. Honor first and always your place on the continuum. From there, your creative energy will flow out most easily and naturally.

But if you're feeling blocked, think about this: Try creating art from some less familiar place. The struggle to create art from alien territory is bound to break things loose.

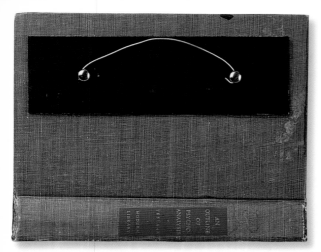

PHOTO 35
Altered book illustrating a brace hanger

book and about ½ inch down from the top and glue. (If you've made the strip out of wood, you'll want to use acrylic medium or contact cement.) Finish by stringing the picture wire between the brad heads or eye screws (photo 35).

BRAD-WIRED HANGER

If your book will hang closed but is heavy, like the It's About Time project on page 40, you can use a hanging mechanism that's essentially the same as the brace method, only without the brace.

For this type of hanger, you'll cut the vertical slits directly into the book's back cover. Mark two spots on the cover, each one approximately 1½ inches down from the top. Place a ruler so it touches both marks and draw a straight line. Find the line's midpoint, and then make two marks on either side, each mark about 2 inches from the line's center. Use the craft knife to cut two vertical slits at these marks. Insert a brad from the outside of the cover to the inside, and open the prongs. Glue the back cover to the page block.

You can then string picture wire from one brad head to the other. In order to hang the book straight, it needs to hang from the book's center of gravity. Put

two nails or picture hangers into the wall so they're 1 inch apart, hang the book's wire on both, and then adjust the book until it hangs straight. The 4 inches of wire you have to work with because of the way you've spaced the brads will give you enough play so you can make those adjustments.

DIRECT LOOP HANGER

If your book will hang closed but is a lightweight volume, you can simply drill holes in the book's back cover. You'll space the holes in the cover just as you did for the brad-wired hanger above. After stringing cord through the holes, tie the ends together on the inside and then glue the back cover to the page blocks. Once again, put two nails or picture hangers into the wall 1 inch apart, hang the cord on both, and then adjust the book until it hangs straight.

DEBRA DRESLER
Viewpoints, 2004
Antique book, original photographs, found objects

Before written text, humans lived in the realm of pictures, both mental and physical. My sculptural wall pieces are my communication tools, used to bridge the gap between our dream world of images and our outer world of written words.

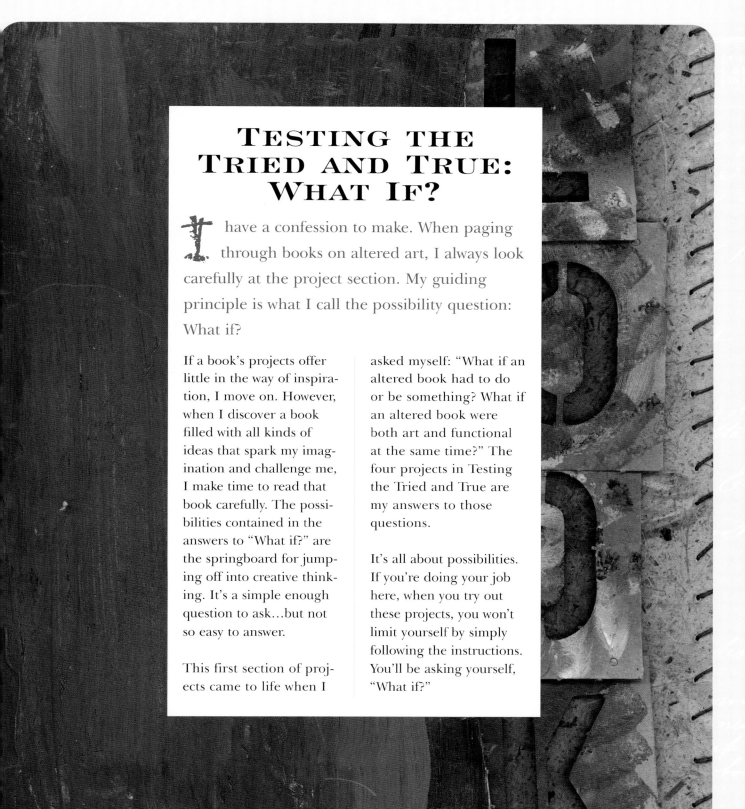

TESTING THE TRIED AND TRUE: WHAT IF?

I have a confession to make. When paging through books on altered art, I always look carefully at the project section. My guiding principle is what I call the possibility question: What if?

If a book's projects offer little in the way of inspiration, I move on. However, when I discover a book filled with all kinds of ideas that spark my imagination and challenge me, I make time to read that book carefully. The possibilities contained in the answers to "What if?" are the springboard for jumping off into creative thinking. It's a simple enough question to ask...but not so easy to answer.

This first section of projects came to life when I asked myself: "What if an altered book had to do or be something? What if an altered book were both art and functional at the same time?" The four projects in Testing the Tried and True are my answers to those questions.

It's all about possibilities. If you're doing your job here, when you try out these projects, you won't limit yourself by simply following the instructions. You'll be asking yourself, "What if?"

Picture This!

Altered books can stand alone as an art form. They need serve no purpose. But they certainly can also combine function with beauty. Here you use a simple childhood staple—a board book—to create an unusual picture frame for that special photograph. This simple project provides a wonderful opportunity for adults and children to collaborate.

MATERIALS AND TOOLS

Photograph
Board book
Metal ruler
Craft Knife
Sandpaper or primer
Decorating arsenal; your choice
Glue
Waxed or release paper
Foam brush
Drill (optional)
Heavy books

INSTRUCTIONS

1. Choose your photograph and a board book with pages large enough so there will be room for a decorative border around the frame opening. For each photograph you frame, you'll need three pages: the first will serve as the frame, the second as the slot page, and the third as the backing.

2. Cut a window in the frame page, (see Cutting Windows and Doors, page 29). The opening should be ½ inch less than both the vertical and horizontal dimensions of the photo. You can center the photo—or not. This is a design decision that's up to you.

3. To make the slot page, use the window you've just cut as a template, and trace the shape onto the board page immediately behind the frame page. Next, add ¼ inch onto each side and to the bottom, and draw this second larger shape on the slot page. Extend the vertical sides of this larger shape all the way up to the top of the page.

4. Use the craft knife to cut out the shape you've just drawn on the slot page. To make sure your photo fits, hold the frame, slot, and the backing pages together tightly, and slide the photograph between the frame page and the slot page until it comes to rest on the bottom of the slot page opening.

5. If you're making a double frame, repeat steps 2, 3, and 4.

6. Next, decorate the outside covers of the book, the border around the frame opening, and the pages (if any) facing the frame page. First, use the sandpaper or the primer and the foam brush to prepare the surfaces you plan to embellish (see Preparing Board Books, page 14).

7. Decorate your book. Be adventurous: drill holes for yarns and dangling beads, or add some 3-D objects. Just make sure nothing gets in between the slot and frame pages.

8. Assemble the frame. First glue the frame page to the slot page and then the slot page to the backing page. If there are any unused pages, now is the time to glue those together as well. Insert the waxed or release paper in between the frame page and the facing page for a single frame or between the two facing frame pages for a double frame, and weigh the project down with a heavy book or two while the glue dries.

My Beauty Comes from Within, But Is My Lipstick on Straight?

Here's a variation on those gifts you used to make at school for your mom—you know, the ones you decorated in her favorite colors or with the flowers she liked the best. It's functional and can be tailored to suit just about anyone's taste. Think vintage buttons and lace for the antique lover, floral themes for the gardener, or sparkle and glitz for those who love bling. No matter what you choose, this mirror is just plain funky fun.

INSTRUCTIONS

 Open your book so it lies relatively flat.

 Cut a niche (see Cutting a Niche, page 31). When creating the page block, don't include the front endpaper; you're going to need it later. The easiest way to draw the niche is to center the mirror on the page block, and trace around it with the pencil. Set the mirror aside. When cutting the niche, keep in mind it needs to be deep enough so the mirror will rest flush with the top of the page block. Don't forget to insert a piece of waxed or release paper between the bottom of the page block and the back cover; you don't want to accidentally glue the block to the cover. Let dry.

3 Decorate the outside covers, the area around the niche, and the surfaces that face the mirror.

4 Next, use the ribbon to create a closure. Cut the ribbon. Insert the end of a length of ribbon in between the endpaper and the front cover. Spread enough glue to attach the endpaper firmly to the inside front cover. Insert the end of a second piece of ribbon in between the back of the page block and the back cover; glue the page block to the inside back cover.

5 Glue the mirror in place. Insert waxed or release paper in between the mirror and the inside front cover, and then close. Use the heavy books or clamps to weigh down the mirror book. Let dry.

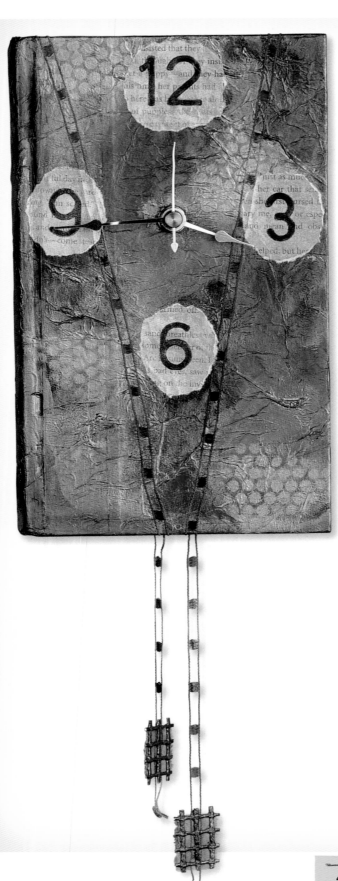

Is It Time Yet?

Here's another functional altered book project that invites you to experiment with decorating techniques. This clock can either hang on the wall or, if the book is thick enough, sit on a shelf. If you're using a thin book, you can simply use the clock mechanism's hanger when you put the clock up on a wall.

MATERIALS AND TOOLS

Clock mechanism (usually 2¼-inches square)*
Book (You'll need one large enough to serve
   as the clock face.)
Metal ruler
Craft knife
Waxed or release paper
Paint or acrylic medium
Decorating arsenal, your choice
Glue
Brads (optional)
Cord, heavy thread, or picture wire (optional)
Nails or picture hangers (optional)
Basic altering tools (page 20)
Drill, with drill bit the same size as the clock
   mechanism spindle (usually a ⅜-inch bit)
* Available at craft supply stores

INSTRUCTIONS

1 Follow the manufacturer's directions to assemble your clock. Be sure to save the packaging, and don't lose track of all the parts until after you've completed the project.

2 After measuring carefully, use the pencil to mark the area on the front cover of the book where you'll center the clock. Drill a hole at the spot where the spindle will need to poke through the cover; make sure the spindle fits through the hole.

3 Determine how many of the pages directly behind the front cover you'll need to embed the clockworks case completely. If you're using a thin book, the mechanism might protrude from the back even after you've cut all the way through the book's pages as well as through the back cover. That's fine. If you've selected a thick book, the niche needs to be just deep enough so the back of the clockworks are flush with the back of the page block opening.

4 Next you'll create the page blocks (see Creating a Page Block, page 31). The first block will consist of the pages immediately behind the front cover where you'll embed the clockworks. If you have any leftover pages, you'll create a second page block. Insert the waxed or release paper in between the front cover and the clockworks page block and also between whatever page block adjoins the back cover and the back cover. You might also need to insert paper between the clockworks page block and a block of unused book pages. Remember: you don't want to glue the back of the clockworks page block to any of the following sections of the book because you'll need to access the back of the mechanism to replace the battery.

5 After checking to make sure that the clock mechanism case is positioned on the clockworks page block so that the spindle will poke through the hole in the front cover, draw a square on the page block that is ¼ inch larger, both horizontally and vertically, than the clock mechanism.

6 Cut a niche in the page block, using the basic altering tools (see Cutting a Niche, page 31). If the book is thin enough that the back of the mechanism protrudes from the back of the page block, you might also need to cut the niche through the back cover so that the cover can close flat. Make sure the clock fits into the opening.

7 Decorate the book covers and page edges in your own personal style. One thing you might try is altering the clock hands that came with the mechanism. Just be sure you don't let any paper or paint even partially block the hole in the center of each clock hand. The holes are cut very precisely to allow the hand to fit over the clock spindle.

8 Decide if you want to put the clock on a shelf or hang it on a wall. If you've decided to hang it and the clockwork's back is accessible through the back cover, just use its hanging mechanism. If not, you'll need to attach a hanging mechanism to the back cover. For a heavier book, you'll want to use the brad-wired hanger (see page 34). If it's a lightweight clock, the direct loop mechanism will work well (see page 34).

9 If you have a page block of unused pages, glue it to the back cover. Let dry. (The clock mechanism will keep the front cover and the clockworks page block together.)

10 Insert the clock mechanism into its niche from the back, and follow the manufacturer's instructions for attaching the hands. Voila! You've created a timeless piece of art that keeps time.

Sacred Spaces

During the final hours of my local public library's book sale, I stood looking over the discards. Once again, the familiar question popped into my head: "what if?" This time, the answer involved the recycling of old book covers to create a small shrine or sanctuary. In constructing this diptych, or two-paneled shrine, you need to think carefully about the size, shape, and number of panels, as well as the direction in which you want to fold them.

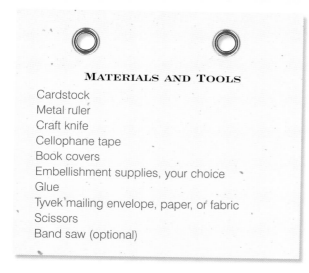

Cardstock
Metal ruler
Craft knife
Cellophane tape
Book covers
Embellishment supplies, your choice
Glue
Tyvek mailing envelope, paper, or fabric
Scissors
Band saw (optional)

INSTRUCTIONS

1. Using the cardstock, plan the design for your triptych shrine panels, and then cut them out carefully. Hinge the center and side panels together with the cellophane tape. Once you've taped the shrine together, take a close look. You may well see things you'd like to change a bit. For example, you may decide you want the side panels to be a different shape or size than the center panel. Now is the time to make your changes.

2. Once you're satisfied with the design, remove the tape from the cardstock. You can now use the pieces of cardstock as the templates for your shrine.

3. Cut the text blocks away from the covers of the book (see Removing a Text Block on page 28). Depending on the size of your panels, you may need more than one book. Save the text blocks pages; they may come in handy for another altered book project.

4. Place the templates onto the book covers, and trace around them. Then re-tape the shrine template back together, so you can refer to the model as you work.

5. Cut the shrine panels out of the book covers. You can do this by placing the book cover on a cutting mat or cardboard and cutting along the lines with your craft knife, using the metal-edged ruler as a guide. If you're lucky enough to have access to a band saw, and you're comfortable using one, cutting the covers with the saw is a quick and easy option.

6. Decide how you want to decorate your panels. Begin by covering the panels completely with at least one layer of decorative papers or glued-on fabric, a coat of paint, or anything else you've found in your decorating arsenal. Make sure you cover all the edges of the panels.

7. Cut the hinges out of a Tyvek mailing envelope, strong handmade paper, or tightly woven, lightweight fabric; they're all good choices. For each side panel that you'll join to the center panel, you'll need two strips, each one 2 inches wide and the same height as the shorter panel (usually the side panel).

8. Position the side panel where you want it. With the panel in the closed position, glue a half of the hinge to the outside of the panel and the other half to the back of the shrine. Let dry. Repeat for the other side panel.

9. Fully open the side panel. You'll find that there is a slight gap between the panels. Bridge the gap by gluing one side of the hinge to the side panel and the other to the center panel. Make sure you use your finger to burnish, or rub, the area where the hinge covers the gap between the panels so you create a slight crease for the inside fold. Repeat for any other side panels.

10. Finish decorating your shrine. Be careful to either make your hinges a design element or cover them completely.

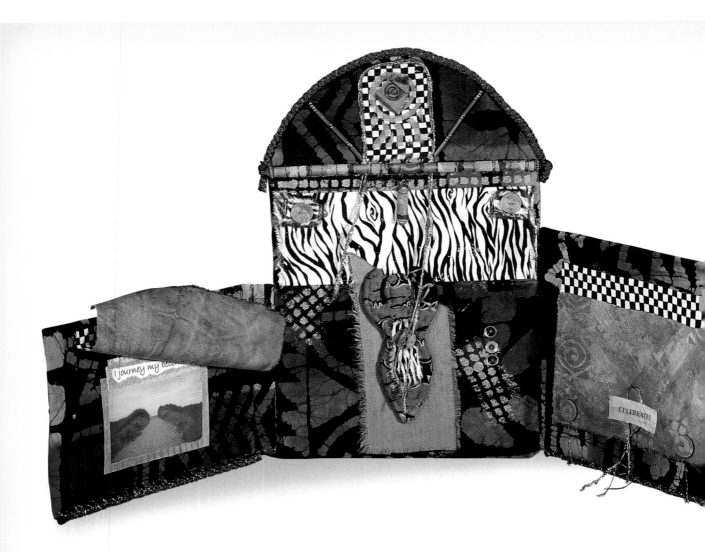

Fabric Shrine

This project offers you a wonderful
jumping-off point to create all kinds of
other variations, both in terms of
decoration and structure.

MATERIALS AND TOOLS

Cardboard
Metal ruler
Craft knife
Book covers
Fabric of your choice
Scissors
Sewing needle and thread
Sewing machine (optional)
Embellishment supplies, your choice

INSTRUCTIONS

1 Plan your fabric shrine with the cardboard template as for the collaged shrine (steps 1 to 5 on page 43), and cut your shapes from book covers.

2 Lay the book cover pieces in correct order, side by side on a sheet of paper. Leave ⅛ inch between the cover pieces. Trace a line, on the paper ¼ inch larger than the outside edges of the covers to create a pattern piece the shape of the shrine you have designed. The extra ¼ inch is your seam allowance.

3 Fold the fabric right sides together, and pin the pattern in place. Cut out the shrine shape.

4 Decorate the front side of each fabric layer, saving any thick or 3D embellishments until you have joined front to back.

5 Lay the shrine shapes, decorated sides together, and hand or machine sew them to each other using the ¼ inch seam allowance on top and sides. Leave the bottom open.

6 Turn right side out and fold the bottom seam allowance to the inside. Sew a line top to bottom along the hinge line where you left the ⅛-inch space in your pattern. This sewn line will secure the bottom fold in place.

7 Complete any additional thick or 3-D embellishing.

8 Slip your cut cover shapes inside the pockets you have created for them between the front and back layers, and hand stitch the bottom closed.

The Art of Teri Edmonds Vodicka

Teri Edmonds Vodicka is making her first altered books. They are books for a special purpose, gifts of love to her father and her husband. She takes us at our word that "there are no rules," that she just needs to go to her art space and make it up.

Teri doesn't create without rules, but the rules she follows are ones she herself made up. For her father's book, there are things she knows before she begins any altering at all: she knows what kind of book she needs to find, that she wants it to be an ABC book so each letter celebrates something about her dad, that she wants to unbind it so she can work flat and take her alterations right off all the edges of the page.

Teri's creative style is goal-oriented, well thought-out, and a great mix of linear left-brain and creative right-brained processing. I suspect that the cohesive, solidly designed work is largely due to the fact that she has followed her natural creative style.

TERI EDMONDS VODICKA
J.E. James Edmonds, 2004
Collage with old dictionary, clip art, scrapbooking paper, electrical and masking tape, waxed paper, family photos; collage, matte transfers, stamping, distressing with ink

This is an ABC format book, created for my Dad as a retirement gift. The background of the "D" page is from an old dictionary and features a dancer (my niece). My Dad loves to shoot craps, so some dice dangle from embroidery floss. If you look closely at the dice, they spell the year 1957 (the year I was born). Dad used to work in construction and his nickname was Dago; unbelievably, the dictionary page had the definition for it, so I highlighted it, along with the word Dad.

TERI EDMONDS VODICKA
Thinking of How Nice You Are, 2004
Collage with clip art, romance novel pages, vintage button card, tissue paper, vintage buttons and ribbons, vintage pictures, family pictures, scrapbooking paper, gesso, watercolors

I made this book as a gift to my husband on our 25th anniversary.

CÉLINE NAVARRO
It's All About Fun, 2004
Children's board book, gel medium, acrylics, gesso, pattern papers, embellishments, collage sheets, stamps, ribbons, pencils, glue

This book is an anthem to childhood, to what makes us the human beings we are now. To life, love, happiness, and fun!

PENELOPE HALL
Jane Eyre, 2004
Copy of *Jane Eyre*, copper mesh, wire, foils used to make new pages, pages built-up with fabric, sections of text, small paintings, beads; pages attached with eyelets and wire, pockets at the front and back hold small prints

What fun to take an old, beaten copy of a classic, read it, and use nontraditional materials to retell the story, following the emotional highs and lows of Jane's life.

CAROL OWEN
Memories, 2004
Paints, napkins, decorative papers, vintage photos, stickers, fibers, found objects, mica; collage, pockets, vellum tip-ins, niches, tags

VICKI SUN
Hollywood: The Way It Was, 2003
Eyelets, Marilyn Monroe's poetry printed on vellum, Marilyn Monroe postage stamp, paints, gold flakes, cocktail napkin, wooden box, tissue paper; stitched, glued, niche cut, painted, fabric transfer

VIVIAN MONTRE
Mother May I?, 2004
Spiderman board book, felt cover, fabric transfers, altered calendar art, clip art, fabric embellishments; deconstructed, sanded, gessoed, oil cloth stitched to edge of each page, stitched together with elastic string

This is an homage to roadside shrines in New Mexico, using images of the Virgin Guadalupe.

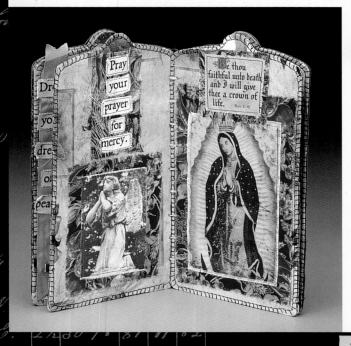

PENELOPE HALL
Abandoned Mines, 2005
Children's book, gold spray paint, glass beads and semi-precious stones strung on wire, acrylic paint, decorative paper, painted flowers, faceted beads, copper wire and garnet bead clasp; tunneled opening carved in each page, painted, embellished

This book's plain cover surrounds a small treasure trove. Each page represents the kind of beauty that is found within plain covers, whether it's a book, a person, a rough gem, or an abandoned place.

CÉLINE NAVARRO
Hidden Love, 2005
Old book, gesso, gel medium, acrylics, mica,
copper mesh, fabric, embellishments, collage
sheets, stamps, pencils, paper bag, cabinet
cards, walnut ink; pages glued, window cut,
copper mesh attached to window, paper bag
aged and used as a pocket

I tend to tell a story when I create. I've been
blessed with the sweetest fiancé on Earth and
this book perfectly translates what I've been
feeling for him for years now. The colors are
pure, sweet, and the materials used are perfect
to tell the softness of our relationship–my feelings for him have been translated mostly
through the process of creation itself.

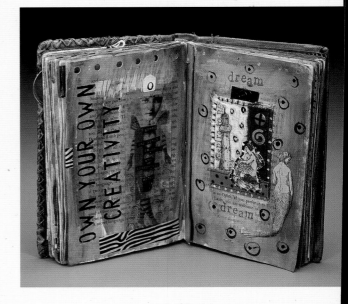

KIM GRANT
Home and Wings, 2004
Acrylics, inkjet transfers, photocopies, collaged and altered photos, acid-dipped copper tape, studs; hand-stitched paper cover, layered, cut windows, gold leaf highlights

STACI ALLEN
Chemical Principles, 2004–2005
Textbook, paint; journaling techniques

The theme for *Chemical Principles* is loosely based upon opposition and explores mostly emotional abstracts. A friend once mentioned to me that she pictured my paintings bound in a book—the thought stuck with me, and I decided to use a book to showcase a series of small paintings.

JOSETTE MARCELLINO
The Gorge in the Glen, 2004
Rubber stamping, altered techniques, artist trading cards, origami, story by artist, pop-ups, tag art, postcard art, collage, pockets made of yuzen

TO BOLDLY GO...

I intended the projects in Testing the Tried and True to entice you into thinking about the possibility of having your altered books fulfill some purpose. In "To Boldly Go", my challenge to you is to think about how you can reshape not only a book's pages but also the book's very shape.

Decorating books in your own unique style will still be important, but the focus in this section is on a new set of possibilities, specifically on how you can integrate the world of more traditional art media—such as textiles, sculpture, and assemblage—with the world of the altered book.

As you page through this section, I also ask that you keep some other things in mind. First of all: know yourself. Pay attention to what feels natural to you as you work. Secondly, never forget that creativity is subjective: it works in different ways for different people. Be aware that what someone else does with a technique or material may not work for you. This is good. It allows our own individuality to claim the piece of art we're making. It pushes us to extend our eyes, our arms, and our thoughts beyond the boxes that contain whatever the au courant expectations happen to be at the time about what makes a beautiful altered book. Those boxes can make it difficult for you to see the whole world of possibilities that only you can discover. My hope is that these projects—and the new thoughts they spark—will awaken your creative spirit so you find yourself thinking in new ways, not just about altered books, but about your creativity in general.

Just Hanging Around

What to do when your shelves, tables, boxes, and studio corners are all filled with altered books? You hang them on the wall. This project also happens to make a particularly unorthodox use of a paper shredder.

INSTRUCTIONS

1 Make a brace hanger out of the book-cover remnant or lightweight cardboard, as described on page 33. Paint one side of the strip in a color that coordinates with the other colors you'll be using. Set it aside to dry for later attachment.

2 Decorate the book's inside covers and the edges that will be visible when you hang the project. You may want to use a small foam brush to paint the surfaces, for example, or cover them with decorative papers.

3 You're going to fold the book's pages to create a symmetrical design on either side of the book's center. You'll begin by working from the back of the book with the last 16 pages. First, count to the fourth page from the back, and draw a cut line ¼ inch in from the page's right edge. (This will serve as the cut line for both the third and fourth pages from the back.) Continue working toward the front, drawing a cut line on every other page, with each line ¼ inch closer to the middle of the book than the one before.

4 Cut the paired pages along the cut lines: you'll be cutting the page with the cut line drawn on it and the one immediately behind it at the same time.

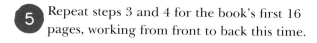

MATERIALS AND TOOLS

Book-cover remnant or lightweight cardboard
Paint
Lightweight book with a solid binding
Decorating arsenal, your choice
2 brads
Picture wire
Glue
Scissors
Bone folder
Paper shredder (optional)
Craft stick

5 Repeat steps 3 and 4 for the book's first 16 pages, working from front to back this time.

6 Now you'll fold the pages to make the design. Begin by placing the book face down and turning to the last page. Fold the top of the page down until it rests in the gutter; sharpen the fold by pressing it with a bone folder. Next fold the page's bottom corner up until it meets the edge of the folded top of the page and forms an off-center point (photo 1). Again sharpen the fold.

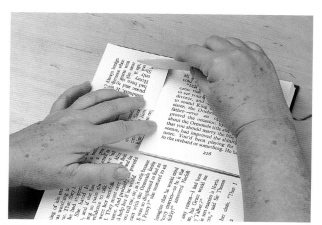

PHOTO 1

PHOTO 2

7 Repeat step 6 with the next page, except this time you'll start by folding the bottom of the page into the gutter, then the top (photo 2). Continue alternating your starting point in this fashion until you've folded all 16 pages. (Initially, the folded pages will form pairs of off-center points. Eventually, however, both the page's top and the bottom will fold all the way into the gutter, forming a point in the middle.)

8 Turn the book face-up, and repeat steps 6 and 7 for the first 16 pages of the book, working from front to back this time.

9 Shred the remaining unfolded pages. You can use a paper shredder if you wish. Insert about three pages at a time, hitting the reverse button to back the paper out when it has gone in as far as it will go. No shredder? Scissor-cut or tear the center pages by hand for a similar effect. It just takes longer.

10 Next, use the scissors to give the shredded pages a haircut. You'll need to decide how you want the center section shaped. I chose to cut the top and bottom short and leave the middle longer. Whatever you do, this is the messiest, wildest part of making this book. It's your chance to be outrageous. The six-year-old inside me loved it! Make sure you fluff the center by gently inserting your fingers in between the clumped pages.

11 Finally, glue the brace hanger in place.

SPRINGBOARD

Hang the book on your wall. Look to see if it needs something else to satisfy your sense of what is right. When I was working on this project, I kept seeing in my mind's eye things dripping out of this book. In my decorating arsenal, I found a piece of multicolored latch hook canvas I had used to stencil fabric. I cut it into a size and shape that spoke to me, positioned the canvas piece at the bottom center of the opened book, and glued it in place between the spine cover and the text block. Adding color-coordinated novelty fibers seemed the perfect finish.

I happen to have a passionate affair with textiles. Now, if I happened to love metals...or had a special affection for found art...something quite different might have found itself dangling from this book.

TIP: There are two things to keep in mind when hanging an altered book on a wall. First, the book's construction and decoration should allow for the necessary hardware so the book can hang properly and securely. Second, picking the right weight book is also important. If the book is too heavy, chances are that the insides will tear away from its covers. So put those encyclopedias and dictionaries away for next time.

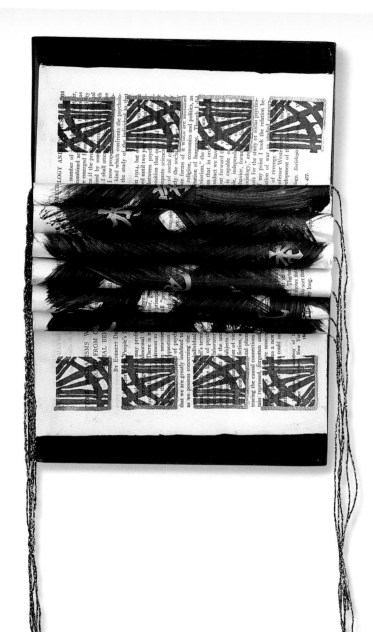

My Roll in Life

The elegant simplicity of this altered book makes it a delicious canvas for your own artistry. The embellishments you choose to define the center rolled section will make it uniquely yours.

MATERIALS AND TOOLS

Book
Decorating arsenal, your choice
Waxed or release paper
Book-cover remnant or lightweight cardboard, brads, picture wire, and strong glue (optional)
Acrylic medium
Glue
Paint, novelty yarn, beads of your choice
Foam brush

INSTRUCTIONS

1 Choose your book carefully. If you plan to hang it, make sure it's a relatively lightweight book. However, even a heavy dictionary is fine if it's going to sit on a shelf or pedestal.

2 Find the book's center. Take the first two right-hand pages, roll their edges away from the center, and insert them into the gutter. Repeat rolling at least two more pairs of pages to the right of your first roll.

3 Repeat step 2 with the first two pages to the left of the book's center. Repeat until you have a total of at least five pairs of rolled pages.

4 Unroll the pages, and mark lightly with a pencil those areas that will show when rolled; don't forget that you'll be able to see all the unrolled pages, the book cover edges, and a small area inside the rolled pages. Now, make your artistic decisions: you can decorate all—or only some— of these elements.

5 Decorate the elements you've decided to embellish. Be careful to protect the sections from each other with waxed or release paper.

SPRINGBOARD

At this point, I urge you to look at what you've done so far and make some additions. In the case of the project pictured on page 55, I painted the edges of the pages, top and bottom, to "frame" the rolled pages. Then I glued fibers to the inside of the rolls so the strings dangle. You could also use beads to make the rolls more dazzling, or you could cut holes that would offer small surprises for the view into the rolled pages. You could even start a second project completely from scratch and come up with an altogether different design that involves some other way to configure the rolled pages. These are just a few of the many variations that are possible.

6 If you're going to hang the book, follow the directions provided in Brace Hanging Mechanism, page 33. Then, glue the brace to the back of the book.

7 Once again, find the book's center. Apply glue to the edges of the first pair of pages to be rolled, and then reinsert the pages into the gutter as you did in steps 2 and 3. Repeat until all the rolled pages are in place.

8 With the book open, create the page blocks by using the foam brush to paint all unrolled page edges with clear-drying acrylic medium. (The pages will be slightly splayed because the book is lying flat.) Let dry.

9 Glue the entire front and back page blocks to the inside covers, if you haven't already accomplished this when you glued the page block edges.

Bend Me, Shape Me

One of my fondest memories as a child in the 1950s was playing with that popular slinking metal-coil toy so many of us owned. When you let it go, it walked down the stairs, flipping itself over and over. I found myself thinking of my old toy while conceptualizing this project. Like the toy, this project is deceptive. While it looks quite complicated, the book is actually a simple construct that invites the artist to move and shape it over and over again.

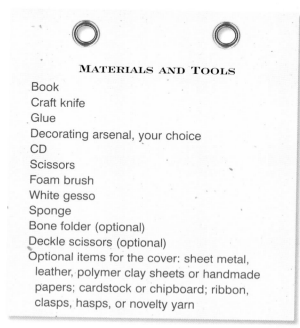

MATERIALS AND TOOLS

Book
Craft knife
Glue
Decorating arsenal, your choice
CD
Scissors
Foam brush
White gesso
Sponge
Bone folder (optional)
Deckle scissors (optional)
Optional items for the cover: sheet metal, leather, polymer clay sheets or handmade papers; cardstock or chipboard; ribbon, clasps, hasps, or novelty yarn

INSTRUCTIONS

1 Use the craft knife to remove the text block from a book (see Removing a Text Block on page 28). Set the cover aside for use in another project.

2 Glue two of the pages from the text together with your favorite glue. Continue gluing pages until you have 26 pairs. (For the best sculptural effect, work with no more than 26 pages. Working with more pages can be a problem, as the book will become increasingly difficult to hold and manipulate. Fewer pages are fine, but you won't get the full range of sculptural variations.)

3 Using the CD as a template, trace a circle on each of the glued-together pages with the pencil, and then cut the circles out with the scissors.

4 Lightly apply gesso on one side of each circle; swiping the circle with a gesso-soaked sponge works fine. When the time comes to decorate the circles, the gesso will allow you to paint, collage, or write on the pages, with the text lightly showing through.

SPRINGBOARD

If you decide you want to glue a separate cover onto the book, you can use any material that can be cut into a pie-shaped wedge. Think sheet metal, leather, polymer clay sheets, and handmade papers: there are so many possibilities! I do recommend stabilizing the book by gluing cardstock or chipboard to the outside page before you glue on any heavier cover materials.

If your covers are especially showy, you'll want a way for the book to stay closed so people can appreciate your artistry. You can simply glue a piece of ribbon between the cover and the cardstock or chipboard backing on the outside of your book. When you tie these ribbons together, the book stays closed. Clasps, hasps, and novelty yarns are other possibilities—or you can take this opportunity to invent something of your own.

5 Next, you'll fold a circle into a pie-shaped wedge. First, fold the circle in half, with the gesso side in. Now open the circle and fold it into equal quarters, again with the gesso side in. Finally fold the circle in half one more time, this time with the gesso side out; this fold line will divide each of two opposing quarters into eighths. Form the pie-shaped wedge by turning the circle so the gesso side faces you, and then bring the two opposing, unfolded quarters toward each other; the quarters that you've folded into eighths should automatically fold in toward the middle as you do this (photo 1). Repeat for all remaining circles. You can use a bone folder to sharpen the folds, if you like.

6 Unfold the circles so you can decorate them with whatever materials from your decorating arsenal inspire you. Make sure you have the pages oriented correctly while you're decorating them; i.e., the folded quarters will be the top and bottom of the pages in your assembled book; the unfolded quarters, the sides.

PHOTO 1
This series demonstrates the folding technique described in step 5, but for simplicity, only a single sheet of paper is folded.

TIP: For your first circle book, I would suggest you skip the art moves and make one out of blank construction paper in order to understand the techniques involved. Once you've mastered them, you can move on to making a decorated circle book.

7 Stack the decorated wedges in the order in which you want them to appear in the book, again making sure they are all oriented correctly. Trust me, you will not be happy if you accidentally glue a page in upside down.

8 Start assembling your book pages in pairs. Glue the right side of the first page back-to-back to the left side of the second page. (Although any quality paper glue will work, I prefer Perfect Paper Adhesive, available on the web and also at craft and art supply stores. It offers the ten seconds of open time needed to position the pages right before it grabs tight and you no longer have to hold it in place.) Next, join the third and fourth pages together in the same fashion, and repeat until you've glued all your pages into pairs.

9 Glue all the pairs together into quartets and then the quartets into octets. Continue until you've joined all the pages together. As the book gets larger, it'll get wiggly. But you will prevail! (Here's an idea: No matter how precise you are, the edges will never exactly match when you join the pages together into a book. Trimming the edges of your pages with deckle scissor and/or painting them will add an interesting visual element while at the same time disguising the mismatched edges.)

10 Decide what you want to do about a cover. The simplest cover is…none at all. You can simply paint or embellish the backs of your first and last pages. If you want something more elaborate, you'll find ideas in Springboard on page 58.

Making a New Kind of Music

This project is another wonderful opportunity to step away from the traditional altered book form and use materials for something other than their intended purpose. Free associate and let your mind wander. See what new uses you can find for altered books made out of CDs.

INSTRUCTIONS

1 First, create a page template for the book. Using one of the CDs, trace two circles on the cardstock with a pencil. Cut out the circles.

2 After drawing a 2 x 4¼-inch rectangle on the leftover cardstock, cut it out. Place the rectangle onto a cardstock circle so that each corner touches the circle's circumference. Trace both of the rectangle's 2-inch sides onto the circle. Cut along both lines. Repeat for the other circle.

3 Join the circles at their straight edges, and tape in place. You now have your template. Each half of the template will be one page in the finished book (figure 1).

4 Trace the template onto a page of the book you're using, and cut it out. Repeat until you have enough paired-circle shapes to make your book. You'll need one more of these paired-circle shapes than the number of internal pages you plan to have. (For example, for a book with 10 pages

MATERIALS AND TOOLS

2 CDs
Scissors
1 sheet of cardstock, any color
Masking or cellophane tape
Book pages, at least 5 x 9 inches (Map or
   atlas pages work especially well.)
Acrylic medium, matte finish
White gesso (optional)
Decorating arsenal, your choice
Sealer or tissue paper
Glue
Ruler
1-inch foam brush
Credit card or bone folder
Sponge
Heavy book

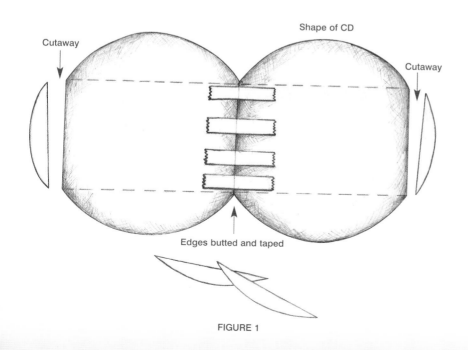

FIGURE 1

plus the covers, you'll need to cut out 11 paired-circle shapes.) Remember that you need to have an odd number of shapes so that the final page will be folded in the correct direction when you attach the covers.

5 Attach the shapes to each other to form the book. Glue the pages to each other in a staggered fashion. For example, you'll glue the left-hand circle of the second shape to the right-hand circle of the first shape, and then the right-hand circle of the second shape to the left-hand circle of the third shape. My method for gluing them together is to apply a thin layer of matte acrylic medium with a foam brush to one page only and then lay the second on top. Smooth out the top page with the edge of a credit card or a bone folder.

6 Continue step 5 until you've joined together all of your paired shapes. At both the front and the back of the book, you'll have an unglued half of a paired shape that you'll use later to attach the covers.

7 Spread the pages out so they lie flat, and either decorate them with whatever materials you've chosen from your decorating arsenal, or apply gesso if you want to use them as journal pages.

8 Next, decorate one side of each CD so it can serve as a cover. Because the CD is plastic and nonabsorbent, be sure to prepare the surfaces first by applying some type of sealer or gluing a layer of tissue to the CD, making sure you use glue such as acrylic medium that adheres well to plastic. This preparation will make it much easier for you to alter the CD surface. How you decorate the CDs is up to you.

9 Fold the book accordion-style. Glue the front cover CD to one end of the accordion, again making sure you've used glue that adheres to plastic. Attach the back cover CD to the other end of the book. Weight the book down with heavy books overnight while the covers are drying.

Free Association at Work

This book came about several years ago as the result of a music-themed altered book round robin. (For more on round robins, see page 120.) While casting about for ideas, I first began thinking about music, and then instruments came to mind, followed by the sound of voices singing. How do we hear these musical offerings? At first, we heard them on records, then on tapes, and now on CDs.

While this series of images was running through my head, I looked over to my junk mail pile, and there was one of those Internet service provider free CDs. That CD posed the first challenge for me as a round robin participant: Could CDs be altered at all? That was followed by a second challenge: Could you turn something as unbook-like as CDs into book pages? In this particular instance, I altered a zippered CD holder and inserted blank CDs for the participating artists to alter. Then I fashioned an accordion CD book to hold the artists' comments and personal information—and out of that accordion book, the Making a New Kind of Music project was born.

Doll + Book = Fun!

I really enjoyed this project. Not only does it combine my love of art dolls and books, it also offers so many different possibilities for both. For me, it's a great example of crossover art, combining as it does two of today's most popular art forms.

INSTRUCTIONS

MAKING THE DOLL'S TORSO AND LIMBS

1 Using the craft knife, cut the text block from your book (see Removing a Text Block, page 28).

2 The text block flanked on both sides by dowels will need to fit within the closed book covers. This means you'll reduce the block's width to compensate for the dowels. To calculate the excess width, first lay the dowels on either side of the text block, and measure the width. This is measurement A. Next, determine measurement B by closing the book and measuring across the width of the cover. Subtract measurement B from measurement A, and add ¼ inch to the difference. That's the extra width that will be cut off the text block.

3 Mark the extra width on the text block with a pencil. Trim the excess from the right side of the block. Don't worry if you cut a little too much.

4 The section of the dowel above the text block will be the outstretched arms; the part below, the legs. Mark on the dowels the lengths you've decided on for the arms, for the torso, and for the legs. (As you can see from the photos, I don't make my arms and legs the same length because I like the sense of movement created by the varied length.) Use the hand pruners to clip off any extra length of dowel.

5 Decorate your dowels. If you're using bamboo, leaving them in their natural state is an option.

6 Using the duct tape, tape the dowels to each side of the text block. Make sure they are centered on the edge of the pages and not placed toward the front or back of the book.

MATERIALS AND TOOLS

Small book (about 3½ x 5 inches, or cut a larger book down to size)

2 dowels, ⅜ x 36 or 48 inches (Wild bamboo works well, too.)

Craft knife

Hand pruners

Decorating arsenal, your choice

Duct tape

Decorative papers or fabric

Glue

Large, flat, clear marble

Picture of a face, cut from a magazine or stamped onto paper (The face needs to be the same size as the flat surface of the marble.)

Clear-drying adhesive

Novelty yarn or other hairlike material

Thick glue, such as fabric glue or an acrylic gel medium

Craft stick

Fabric scrap of lightweight material for the doll's turban

Painted (optional) 2-inch-square scrap leather or canvas-weight fabric

Heavy thread or sinew

Sturdy, flexible paper, or fabric (for the double-page spread)

Tyvek mailing envelope

Foam brush (optional)

Scissors

Pushpin

7 Glue decorative papers or fabric to the top, bottom, and right side of the torso to hide the tape. Set aside.

MAKING THE DOLL'S HEAD AND NECK

1 Use a clear-drying adhesive to glue the picture of the doll's face to the marble's flat side, and smooth out any bubbles you see. (Any unevenness in the marble can cause distortion, so the flatter, the better.)

2 Lay the strands of novelty yarns or any other fibers you've chosen to represent hair across the middle third section of the back of the marble.

3 Use a thicker glue to attach the craft stick to the back of the face marble (photo 1). Play with the positioning; for example you may want to tilt the face a bit. Let it dry. (You can use this time to work on the inside of the book or decorate the cover.)

4 Glue one corner of the fabric scrap to the craft stick and then wrap the fabric over the top of the marble into a turban shape.

5 Do you want to paint or cover the neck in any way? If so, do it now.

6 Cut the leather or the canvas-weight fabric so it's just a tiny bit larger than the back of the marble. Apply the thicker glue to the back of the leather piece or fabric and glue it over the craft stick and fibers to the back of the marble.

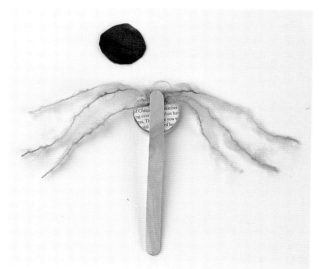

PHOTO 1

FINISHING THE DOLL'S TORSO

1 With materials from your decorating arsenal, decorate the outside of the book covers, the edges, and the ⅛ inch or so of the inside front and back covers that will show when you assemble the doll.

2 Using the heavy thread or sinew and the pushpin, make a direct loop hanger on the back cover of the book (see Direct Loop Hanger on page 34).

3 Next, you'll make the double-page spread. Out of the sturdy, yet flexible, paper, cut a rectangle the same height as your text block and wide enough to stretch all the way across inside the front cover and the doll's torso, when it's been placed between the book covers. Cut a piece of a Tyvek mailing envelope to the same size, and glue it to the back of the paper.

4 Fold the paper in half to mark where the gutter will fall. Again, raid your decorating arsenal, and decorate your spread. If you want to add a collage, words, or even a story to the spread, now's the time. Set it aside.

ASSEMBLING THE DOLL

1 Position the craft stick, and glue it to the inside of the back cover between the holes you've made for your hanger.

2 Cover the back of the text block/torso with glue, and then attach it to the inside back cover over the craft stick.

3 Finally, attach the double-page spread. Glue the spread's left side to the inside front cover, making sure the fold in the middle lines up with the book's gutter. Glue the spread's right side to the torso.

VARIATION
A Standing Doll

Do you want to make a standing doll instead of one that hangs on a wall? No problem: just embed one of the doll's dowel-legs in a heavy block.

INSTRUCTIONS

1. Make the doll with one leg longer than the other. Center the doll over the block you're using as a base, and with a pencil or pen mark where the longer leg touches the base. Drill the hole. Make sure a scrap piece of dowel fits snugly into the hole.

2. Decorate your base.

3. Use glue (such as contact cement or an acrylic gel medium) to attach the metal bolt nuts or other metal hardware to the base as shown in photo 1. (Remember: the taller the figure, the heavier the base must be to keep the doll upright and balanced.)

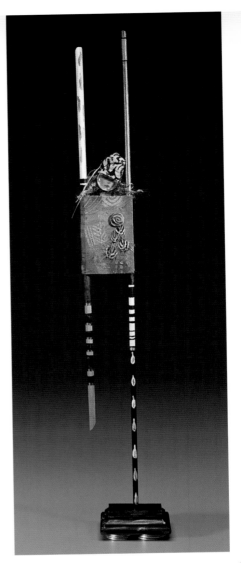

4. Fill the drilled hole with white craft glue. Insert the doll's longest dowel leg into the hole, and use the rag to wipe away the excess. (You might need to whittle the leg a bit to make it fit.) Make sure the torso is centered on the base. Brace in place until the glue dries by placing the doll against something so it doesn't lean. That's all it takes!

MATERIALS AND TOOLS

Scrap piece of dowel
Block of wood
Decorating arsenal, your choice
Metal bolt nuts or other metal hardware
Contact cement or acrylic gel medium
White craft glue
Drill, with a ⅜-inch bit
Pencil or pen
Rag
Whittling knife (optional)

Where Are My Socks?

So just where are my socks? "In my altered book," some artists might answer. There is something about the textures of textiles that seem to inspire and entice a lot of us. They invite a new level of decoration, they are infinitely flexible, and you don't even have to be an expert at sewing to excel.

INSTRUCTIONS

1. Use the craft knife to remove the text block from a book with covers that are at least as tall and wide as the pages you're planning for your fabric book (see Removing a Text Block on page 28). Set the text block aside for use in another project.

2. Cut the fabric for your cover. It will need to extend ½ inch beyond the book cover on four sides.

3. Glue the fabric to the outside of the cover by using either the fusible web (directions come with the web) or by applying the sheet adhesive to the cover and then smoothing the fabric onto it. Next, fold the points in at the corners, and glue them to the inside of the cover. Finish by gluing the ½-inch border over the cover's edges.

4. Measure the book cover's length from top to bottom and its width from the center of the spine to the cover's edge. Cut a piece of fabric to these dimensions for each book page, plus an extra piece the same size for the binding flap. Each rectangle becomes two consecutive pages when it is folded in half, wrong sides together, after the page has been decorated, and the backs are fused or sewn together.

5. Pin page numbers to the fabric. On each fabric rectangle, the left half will be the odd number and the right half the even numbered page. Numbering the pages will help you keep track of which pages face each other. As you embellish the fabric, keep ½ inch unembellished on both left and right edges of the rectangle. These areas need to be free for binding the book pages together.

6. Decorate the front sides of each rectangle with materials from your decorating arsenal. Save 3-D additions until after the page is folded and the wrong side/back of the fabric has been fused or sewn together. While it looks like a 'spread' when the rectangle is layed out flat, remember that

MATERIALS AND TOOLS

- Book
- Craft knife
- Scissors
- Metal ruler
- Fabric
- Sheet adhesive, fusible web, or needle and thread
- Decorating arsenal, your choice
- Thread, buttons, zippers, eyelets (optional)
- Iron and padded surface
- Pins
- Sewing machine (optional)
- 2 large bulldog clips
- Stapler or grommets (optional)

these pages will not face each other. Page two, for example will face page three after the folding and fusing. Complete your page decoration.

7. Connect your pages back-to-back, using fusible web, sheet adhesive, or hand sewing. Also think about buttoning or zippering them together. How about using eyelets?

8. Assemble the pages by stacking them on top of each other, making sure they are in the right order. Use bulldog clips or a few stitches to tack the pages together.

9. The flap piece serves to attach the text block to the covers. Fold the middle third of the flap piece around the raw spine edge of the page stack. Make sure the front side of the fabric is facing the text block. Stitch through all layers to secure them. If sewing is not your thing, use any method—such as stapling, gluing, or using grommets—to first attach each page to each of its neighbors and then secure the flap around the text block as shown on page 69, using glue instead of stitches. Secure with clamps and let dry.

10 Apply adhesive to the wrong side of the flap, and attach the flap to the front cover. Repeat for the back cover.

11 Cut two fabric pieces to cover the inside front and back covers. Attach each of these fabric pieces onto an inside cover over the flap you've just glued down.

12 Now you can decorate the inside pages with the heavier 3-D adornments. You can also decorate your cover with materials from your decorating arsenal.

A Natural Partnership?

Of all the artists who have crossed over into altered books from other media, fiber artists seem to have made the easiest transition. It could be that you can do similar things with paper and fabric. After all, quilters are already telling their stories through journal quilts. Whatever the reasons, for many fiber artists, altering books seems a natural step to take in their creative journey.

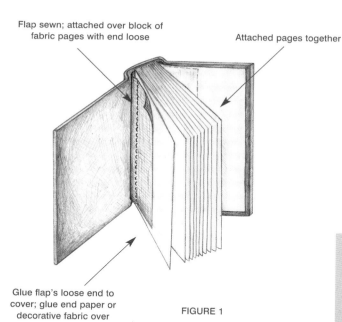

Flap sewn; attached over block of fabric pages with end loose

Attached pages together

Glue flap's loose end to cover; glue end paper or decorative fabric over flap/cover

FIGURE 1

SPRINGBOARD

Instead of your book's pages having raw edges, they can have finished edges, as shown in the photograph above. You just need to be willing to do a little sewing. When cutting out the fabric for the pages, double the page width you determined in step 4, and then add 1 inch to the top-to-bottom measurement. Decorate and embellish the pages, reserving a ½ inch at both the top and bottom for the seam. When you've finished decorating, fold the width in half with the decorations on the inside. You can either glue or sew a ½-inch seam along the top and the bottom of the page.

Books to Make Your Heart Sing

This project is "assemblage meets altered books." It sits on a shelf, open or closed. You'll decorate the covers and create a spread of facing pages that includes a niche. That niche, when filled with whatever makes your heart sing, can be an absolutely personal creative expression.

MATERIALS AND TOOLS

Book
Craft knife
Acrylic medium in matte or soft gel
Waxed or release paper
Decorating arsenal, your choice
Glue
Foam brush
Collection of some of your favorite objects
   to put in the niche
Small objects to serve as fillers for your
   composition
Heavy books or clamps

INSTRUCTIONS

1. Choose your book. It must be thick enough to create a niche in which your collection of 3-D objects can nestle and still allow the cover to close.

2. Cut the niche deep enough to hold the objects you've selected (see Cutting a Niche on page 31). As you can see from my typography book, you don't have to stop at one niche. I cut a second, shallower niche and filled it with bamboo.

3. With materials from your decorating arsenal, decorate the outside covers, the inside front cover, and the border around the niche. If any of the area behind the objects in the niche will show, decorate that as well. Consider decorating the outside edges of your text block as well.

4. Your goal is to pack the inside of the niche completely. Arrange—and then rearrange—the objects inside the niche until you're satisfied. Now glue them down. Keep in mind that in addition to your favorite objects, you'll need to find or create fillers that complement your collection and insert them into any empty spaces. (In my project, the fillers that called to me were lengths of bamboo.)

5. Check the overall effect. Tweak, as needed.

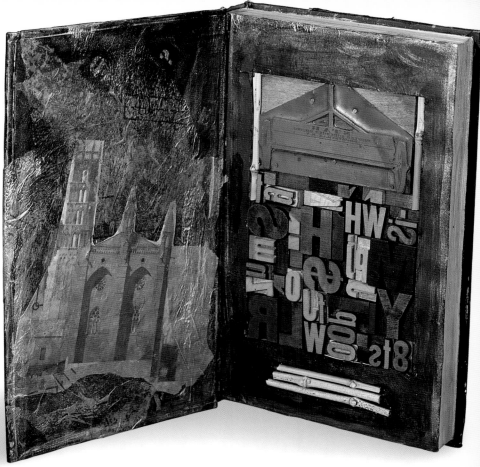

SPRINGBOARD

You'll find there is nothing like working with something you really love to help you tap into your creative wellspring. My version of this project is filled with my love of typography and old printing processes.

But what if you filled a book niche with shells and polished beach glass brought back from that last beach walk, or you used mementos to mark a special occasion? Old photos and small pieces of ephemera might celebrate your family heritage. My latest idea is to draw on my grandson's little toy car fixation and make a car assemblage for his room. As you can see, possibilities are endless.

Celebration!

This altered book is an artful way to celebrate a life—yours, a family member's, or a special friend's. I love the design and sturdiness of this book. Constructed entirely of book covers and hinges, this project can fold together into a book or be opened up for display—and you can choose to display a single frame, a few selected pages, or the entire book. Whether you make this for yourself or for someone else, this altered book offers special glimpses into someone's life and thoughts.

INSTRUCTIONS

1 First, you'll make a small paper model out of copy paper. Trust me, as you assemble and decorate the actual book, you'll refer to your model a lot! Begin by deciding how many panels you want. Make sure it's an even number so your front and back covers will be properly aligned when you fold the book together. (I'd recommend 6, 8, or 10.)

2 Now cut strips from the long side of ordinary copy paper, each measuring 2 x 11 inches. (Two should be enough, but you can cut more if necessary.) Fold the first strip accordion-style, as shown in the figures on page 79. If you're planning on more panels, fold a second strip, overlap it with the first, and tape them together. Cut away any extra panels, and mark the top and bottom on the front panel.

3 Decide where you want your windows. Use the craft knife to cut the window openings into the model's panels. I like to make a full opening with a proportional border (photo 1). You might want to create triangles or slats. It's up to you.

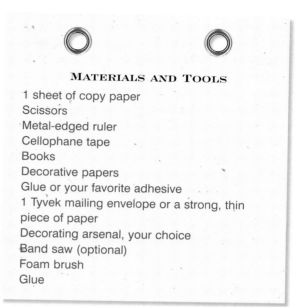

MATERIALS AND TOOLS

1 sheet of copy paper
Scissors
Metal-edged ruler
Cellophane tape
Books
Decorative papers
Glue or your favorite adhesive
1 Tyvek mailing envelope or a strong, thin piece of paper
Decorating arsenal, your choice
Band saw (optional)
Foam brush
Glue

4 Now you're ready to start on the project itself. Remove the text blocks from discarded books until you have enough covers for your panels (see Removing a Text Block, page 28). Save the text blocks for a future project.

5 Mark the dimensions of your panels on the covers with the ruler and pencil. Cut out the panels. Using a band saw—if you're comfortable with handling one—will make this task go quickly.

6 Refer to your model to determine how many panels will have a window opening. Cut out the windows (see Cutting Windows and Doors, page 29).

7 Cover all the edges of your panels with decorative papers, using glue and the foam brush. (You'll complete the final decorating once the panels are hinged together.)

PHOTO 1

⑧ Cut hinge strips that are about 1½ inches wide and the height of the panels out of the Tyvek mailing envelope or a thin, strong piece of paper. You'll need one fewer hinge strips than the number of panels in your book.

⑨ Next, attach the hinges (see figure 1). Lay your panels down, side by side, making sure they're in the correct order. Fold the hinge strips in half lengthwise; glue the left half of the hinge to the top right side of each panel except the last one. Let dry. Flip the entire row of panels over; the unglued half of each hinge should be showing. Glue the loose edge of each hinge along the top of the adjoining hinge, making sure the hinge fits tightly to both of the panels. Repeat for all panels. Let dry.

⑩ Open the panels so they're flat, and decorate them. Remember that every window will potentially frame an image on each adjoining panel, depending on how the book is configured. Before you glue an image down, make sure it's clearly visible through any window panel that will possibly act as its frame.

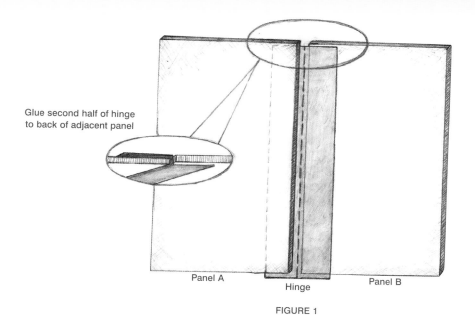

Glue second half of hinge
to back of adjacent panel

Panel A   Hinge   Panel B

FIGURE 1

Welcome to My World

This altered book is not only a celebration of life, it also offers a chance to remind ourselves of what we love and treasure—colors, images, textures, words—anything that is most precious and sacred to you. For me, creating this book offered a chance to take an unexpected and delightful journey of rediscovery.

Not sure where to start? Here are some questions to ask yourself.
• What energizes my life?
• What stimulates my creative life?
• What makes me content?
No doubt as you think about these questions, other ones will surface.

Record Your Thoughts

To identify the images and words that mean the most to you, you need only pay attention to what pops into your consciousness. Writing, drawing, and sketching are helpful exercises.

Still stuck? Here are some more activities that might help:
• Take a walk. Even better, walk somewhere you've never been before. What do you notice? What do you find?
• Listen to your favorite music. Think about what images, feelings, colors, and memories come to you.
• Watch or—even better—play with a child. Leave your self-consciousness at the door, and jump right in.
• Plan an evening or afternoon for YOU. Take your solitary self and do whatever it is you like to do—enjoy a special activity, visit specific places, eat certain foods—anything that lifts your spirits.
• Write down all the favorite things you can think of.

Find Your Theme

In looking over what you've recorded, see what images and themes emerge. Now, if you notice wings on humans wearing dunce caps (an image that occurs with some regularity in altered book projects these days), then that's your personal icon to use in your art ...but I'll bet you'll find something ever so much more uniquely yours. Use the elements that most celebrate you.

Gather your materials and begin working. Remember: those written and visual answers you've recorded are great art materials themselves...collage them right in.

For me, images of trees, textures, carving stamps, exploring, music, and earth colors kept recurring. I used them all while creating my book.

Now, what will yours look like?

Standing on Its Own

Displayed on a shelf or table, this altered book becomes your own personal interpretive sculpture. It can be many things: a memento of a treasured experience or a representation of something or someone important to you. It's also a wonderful gift for that special friend, parent, or relative.

INSTRUCTIONS

1. Design your 3-D collage. For your first project, it's probably best to plan on no more than three layers plus a background. Decide how far apart you want the layers, and how high, wide, and deep the space for the collage needs to be. The simplest way to do this is to cut out the images you plan to use and arrange them as a flat composition on a piece of scrap paper. Draw a line around the composition with the pencil and measure its width and height; the depth is determined by the thickness of the book.

2. Insert waxed or release paper between the front cover and the text block. Then insert release paper between the pages of the book wherever you intend to place an image.

3. Using the acrylic medium, foam brush, and heavy books or clamps, begin the process of gluing each group of pages that are in between release papers into page blocks. (See Creating the Page Block on page 31.)

4. While you're waiting for the page blocks to dry, attach the elements you're going to use for your collage to the cardstock with glue. Cut them out, leaving a cardstock tab or two on each to glue into the book between the page blocks. Two tabs will make for a more stable element in the finished collage.

MATERIALS AND TOOLS

Images to use in the collage
Scrap paper
Thick book
Waxed or release paper
Acrylic medium
Cardstock
Glue
Decorating arsenal, your choice
Objects to serve as feet and ornament for
  the top (Think dice, cords, toggle buttons,
  rocks, or shells.)
Paint
Scissors
Craft knife

5 Next, mark how large a niche opening you want. Keep the release papers in place just while you're creating the text blocks so you don't glue the different layers to each other. Cut the niches in all the text blocks and in the front cover, following the process described in Cutting a Niche on page 31.

6 Decorate the covers and the background behind the last niche opening. Now is the time to decorate the feet as well as any objects you might want to place on top of your book.

7 Working from the last page block to the first, glue the tabbed images into the niche openings. They will be glued between two text blocks. Let Dry.

8 Glue the front and back covers to their adjoining page blocks, and then paint the page edges as you would to create a page block. This will seal your book closed. Let dry.

9 If you wish, glue any decorative objects you've chosen to serve as feet or as a decoration for the top of the book.

Well, Why Not?

I think there is a subversive rebel in me, one that all too often asks, "Well, why not?!" or "Why does it have to be this way?" or "So, what if...?" This almost never gets me into trouble when I'm doing my art. In fact, it often leads me on a fantastic journey out of the box.

With this particular project, I asked myself, "Why does a collage have to be flat?" In my mind, I saw a miniature stage set: mountains and trees behind an old house. Sitting in the middle of the sidewalk leading up to the house is a cat. There are also props and actors waiting to begin their roles. Framing this scene and its inhabitants is a stage, complete with scrim and curtain.

This idea inspired Standing on Its Own, a 3-D collage, where layers of flat art overlap to reveal a scene, a kind of stage set in a book. Layering your scene can be fun, simple—and maybe even profound, if you're having a profound sort of day.

Now, in my example, the collage was a picturesque mountain scene. Maybe in your mind, you see a vintage photograph or an abstract (like the one I actually created as a sample art piece for this project). The point is that this collage can be almost anything you can draw up from your creative wellspring.

The World Is My Canvas

Are you ready for something more challenging than simply embellishing pages in your altered books? Are you asking yourself, "What is possible?" How about making your own books? Why not? *The World Is My Canvas* is Penny Baugh's greatly simplified version of a concept that originated from North Carolina mixed media artist Jane Powell.

INSTRUCTIONS

1 Measure your stretched canvases. (Instead of two canvases, you can use one canvas and one old book cover.) Subtract ⅛ inch from the cover's width and height, and cut six pages from an old book to those dimensions. Because you'll decorate the pages in some manner, you may want to strengthen the pages (see Preparing Sewn Signature and Perfect Bound Books, page 14).

2 Next make the accordion-binding spine. First, cut the watercolor or pastel paper so it is four times the width of your cover and ¼ inch less than its height. Fold the watercolor paper in half lengthwise. To sharpen the crease, press the fold with the bone folder.

3 Fold the paper accordion-style, as shown in figure 1, until there is less than an inch between the valley (a V shape) and the mountain (an inverted V) in your strip. When completed, your strip will consist of seven mountains and eight valleys. Set the strip aside.

4 Cut six pages from heavy paper or doubled book pages. Each page should be the height of the accordian strip and slightly narrower than the canvas cover. Use the pencil to mark the top of

MATERIALS AND TOOLS

2 small stretched canvases, 5 x 7 inches or smaller, or 1 prestretched canvas and 1 book cover
Old book pages to use as inside pages
Watercolor or pastel paper
Decorating arsenal, your choice
Glue
Transparency film (optional)
Acrylic adhesive
Waxed or release paper
Upholstery-weight fabric or leather
Thick glue or double-sided tape
Ruler
Pencil
Scissors
Bone folder
2 clamps (must be able to open to four times the depth of your prestretched canvas)

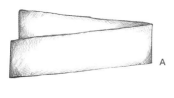
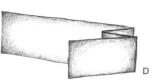

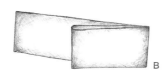
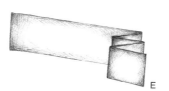

FIGURE 1

the first valley, or V-shaped fold, of your accordion-binding strip. Carefully insert your first page and press in place. (I recommend using Perfect Paper Adhesive; it allows you just enough time to reposition the page but then sets quickly and firmly so you can move on.) Repeat until you've attached all six pages.

9 Attach the covers. First, decide if you want the niches to face in or out. If you're using a slower-drying glue, place a sheet of waxed or release paper between the pages and the cover. Glue the loose edge of the binding strip to the right side of the inside front cover. (If you've decided to use the niche as an inside cover, you may want to trim the width of the tail ends of the binding strip before gluing; this prevents the strip from slipping over the niche.) Repeat for the back cover. Cover the binding strip with collage or trim, if you like.

10 Cut the upholstery-weight fabric or leather so it will cover the entire spine and wrap it around to the book's front and back covers. The spine cover's length and shape is yours to decide.

11 Use the clamps to close the book tightly and hold it in place. (Be careful not to put the clamps where you'll be placing the spine cover.) Apply the thick glue or a sheet adhesive onto the back of your spine cover. Starting from the front cover, wrap the strip over the spine and then onto the back cover. Press the strip firmly against the spine to ensure a solid bond. Leave clamped for several hours.

12 When the book is dry, you might want to add extra touches, such as heavier 3-D objects, or even a little extra dab of color.

your pages and the binding edge; you might also want to number them. This will help you maintain continuity as you work.

5 Decorate both sides of each page. Make sure the spine sides of your pages are free of any bulky embellishments. Decide whether you want to color your folded binding strip so it coordinates with your pages.

6 Now, turn your attention to the covers. Apply materials from your decorating arsenal to all the surfaces of your canvases. The goal is to cover all edges as well as the back and the front. You may choose to layer with napkins, tissue, paints, and stamps. Overlapping your elements is a great idea. Save any heavier 3-D embellishments for later.

7 Turn your canvases over so the open back of the canvas faces you, giving you two niches to work with. If you wish, you can put 3-D objects inside, either by gluing them down or holding them in place with a piece of transparency film so they can rattle in the niche.

8 You're ready to bind your pages together. Apply the acrylic adhesive to the right side of

VARIATION

A Travel Journal

Here's a variation on *The World Is My Canvas* book that makes the best functioning travel journal I have yet come across for artists like us. You get absolute portability, plus the chance to play with all your decorative, assemblage, bookbinding, and altered book-decorating tricks.

NOTE:

Instead of inserting individual pages in your accordion binding as you did in *The World Is My Canvas*, you'll make little pamphlets out of individual flat signatures from paper you can write or draw on. You'll cover each set of signatures in decorative papers cut from an old book. While on your trip, you can tuck these pamphlets into your pocket or daypack and record your experiences as you go. You can always reserve one signature for brilliant ideas that come to you as you wander, and then use the rest to record experiences and hold photos of your journey.

When you get back, decorate the pages with mementos, photos, found objects you've collected…and then do the final assembly by inserting an entire pamphlet into each accordion pleat. While these instructions call for binding five of these pamphlets together into a travel journal, you can always make more signatures if you're a prolific sketcher or going on a longer trip. You can make several volumes, or you can extend the accordion strip and make a fatter book.

INSTRUCTIONS

1 First, you'll create a template that you'll use when you sew the page signatures together. Fold the cardstock in half lengthwise. Measure and mark the center of the fold. Next, measure and mark on the fold a point 1½ inches in from each end. Set the template aside.

2 Cut 25 pieces out of your writing paper and five pieces of the paper from the old book or map. Each piece should be the same length as the stretched canvas and twice its width.

3 Fold all the pages in half widthwise, using the bone folder to sharpen the fold. The folded pages should now be the same length and width as your covers.

4 You're going to create piles of paper; each pile will have one piece from the old book or map and five pieces of the writing or sketching paper. Stack the paper with the piece cut from the old book or map on the bottom.

5 After making sure the first stack is aligned, lay it so the fold's entire length rests on the foam core or cardboard. Place the centerfold of the cardstock template on the fold in the paper

6 Using the pushpin or awl, make a hole through all the layers at each of the three points you've marked on the cardstock template.

7 Now, you'll sew your signature together. Carefully lift the stack off of the foam core or cardboard. Thread the large-eyed needle with the waxed linen thread. Working from the outside of the pamphlet, insert the needle into the paper's center hole and pull through, leaving a tail. Next, bring the needle back out through the bottom hole. Now, again working from outside the pamphlet, insert the needle through the top hole, and finally bring it back up through the middle hole. Tighten or adjust the thread, if necessary. Cut the thread, leaving enough to tie a knot with the tail (figure 1).

8 Repeat steps 5, 6, and 7 with the remaining five stacks of paper. These are the pamphlets you take on your trip.

9 After you've come back from your travels, refer back to *The World Is My Canvas* project (on page 78), and complete step 3 and then 6 to 12.

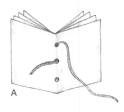 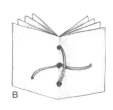 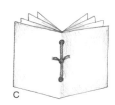

A   B   C

FIGURE 1

The Art of Kristin Smith

Kristin Smith, who lives in Jacksonville, North Carolina, embodies for me what book altering at its best could be for every one of us. One thing she proves is that formal art training is not a prerequisite. She just plain explores what can happen when she uses her books and art materials. She thinks "book," picks up something as mundane as a receipt book from her part-time job selling used children's clothes, and makes art out of it. Her guiding principles are: "Does it mean something to me?" and "What can I do with this?"

I remember asking her once, "How do you make sealing watercolor oil pastels with acrylic matte medium work?" Her answer: "Well, it does peel a lot. I just don't worry about it. Add another layer of something…Interesting things might happen." Out of her happy accidents, Kristen creates original art, uses her original words, and laughs at herself a lot. Her art is here because her creative spirit inspires me so.

KRISTIN SMITH, *Strange Birds in the Tree of Heaven*

KRISTIN SMITH, *Receipt Book*

KRISTIN SMITH, *The Book Formerly Known as Hairdo*

DEBRA DRESLER
Holding it All Together, 2004
Antique book, original photographs, found objects;
designed to hang on the wall

DIANE CASSIDY
American Ghosts, 2002
Found images; altering, coloring, high-
lighting, sanding

I had fun emphasizing the ghostliness
of the book by the insertion of a 10-sec-
ond recording of myself wailing; it's
activated when you poke at the ghost's
eye on the cover.

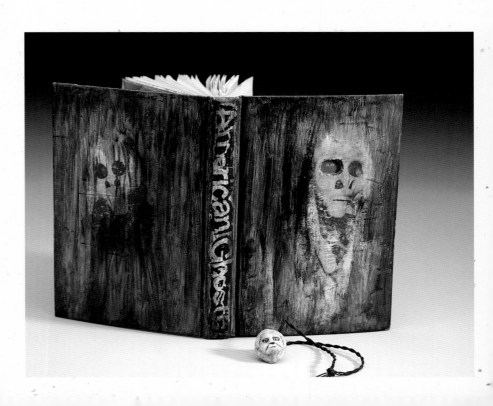

Adam
Cast
Forth

The Garden
Was it real
or
was it a dream
Slow in the
hazy light
I have been
asking
Almost as a
comfort
if the past
belonging to
this now
unhappy Adam
was nothing
but a magic
fantasy of
that God
I dreamed.
now it is
imprecise
in memory
that lucid
paradise
but I know
it exists
and will
persist though
not for me
The unforgiving
earth is my
affliction and
the incestuous
wars of Cains
and Abels and
their progeny.
Nevertheless
it means much
to have loved,
to have been
happy,
to have
touched upon
the living
garden
even for
one day.

Jorge
Luis
Borges

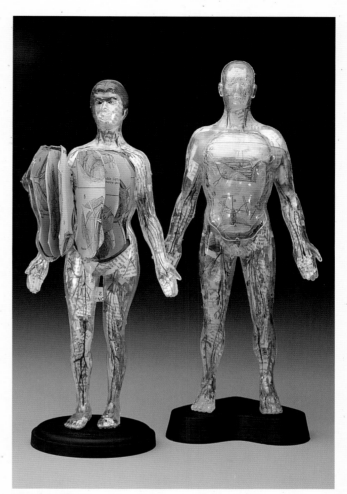

MIRIAM SCHAER
Body of Knowledge, 2002
Plastic figures, dye, linen thread;
book created and figure lined with
text from the *Atlas of Surgical
Operations*

ELENA MARY SIFF
Adam Cast Forth, 2003
Carob pod, gold and silver paper, poem by
Jorge Luis Borges titled "Adam Cast Forth"

STACI ALLEN
The Speed of Dark, 2005
Paperback book, faux suede, three-dimensional
objects; spine cut off, book divided into sections,
each section bound with faux suede, holes punched
into binding, pages tied together, fold-outs, tags

The Speed of Dark is a narrative, set slightly in the
future, about an autistic man. He has to make a
decision between accepting a new surgery that can
correct his autism, but potentially destroy who he
was before. The story deals with the story of split
personalities within oneself, and the artwork reflects
this dichotomy.

CORINNE STUBSON
Not Your Type, 2005
Vintage typewriter base, two books, circular drain plate, molding-foam clay, paper, yarn, paint, tongue depressors, decorative art papers, stick-on typewriter letters, toy compass, adhesives

CORINNE STUBSON
The Bookplate: Food for Thought, 2005
Plastic plate, book, fabric, yarn, decorative art paper, acrylic paints, acrylic gel medium, glue, copy machine, slice of wheat bread, iron-on vinyl, onion skins

JANET HOFACKER
My Friend Arielle, 2003
Fabric, handmade cloth; sandwich technique,
photo transfer, triptych-style fold out

RHIAN BEBB
Soft…Hard, 2005
Metal, rubber matting, netting, paper, glass stone,
cardboard slide holders formed into accordion books
to fit in niches

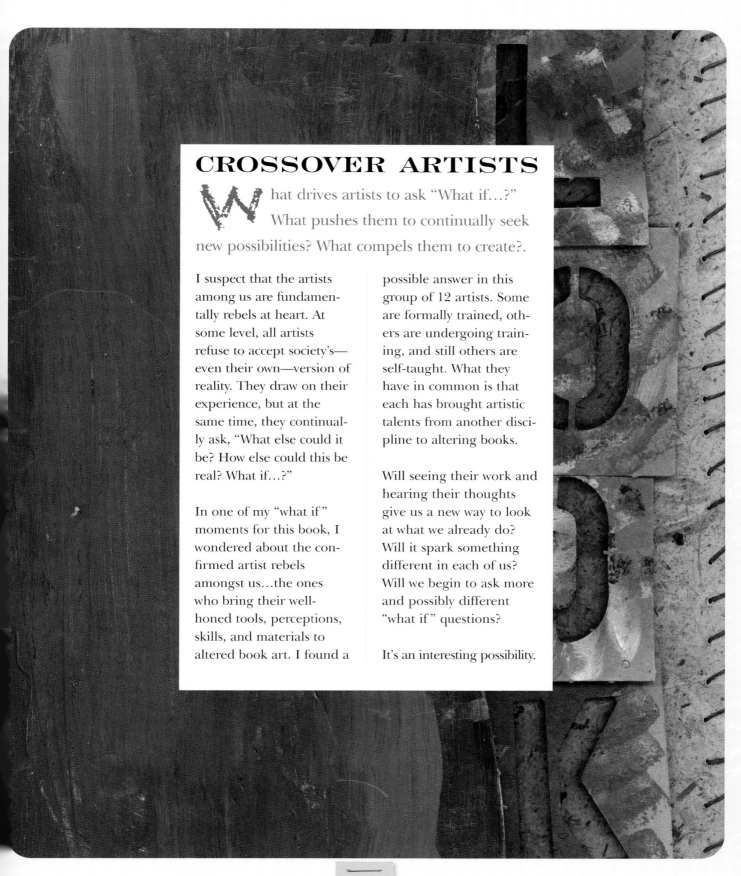

CROSSOVER ARTISTS

What drives artists to ask "What if…?" What pushes them to continually seek new possibilities? What compels them to create?.

I suspect that the artists among us are fundamentally rebels at heart. At some level, all artists refuse to accept society's— even their own—version of reality. They draw on their experience, but at the same time, they continually ask, "What else could it be? How else could this be real? What if…?"

In one of my "what if" moments for this book, I wondered about the confirmed artist rebels amongst us…the ones who bring their well-honed tools, perceptions, skills, and materials to altered book art. I found a possible answer in this group of 12 artists. Some are formally trained, others are undergoing training, and still others are self-taught. What they have in common is that each has brought artistic talents from another discipline to altering books.

Will seeing their work and hearing their thoughts give us a new way to look at what we already do? Will it spark something different in each of us? Will we begin to ask more and possibly different "what if" questions?

It's an interesting possibility.

ANNE MAYER HESSE,
DOLLMAKER

I first met contemporary art doll artist Anne Mayer Hesse long before altered books had entered either of our creative lives. At the time, she was exhibiting solely as a mixed-media doll artist. In its earliest incarnation, the journal doll pictured here came from an idea Anne had while participating in a professional doll artists' collaboration. She surprised us all with her idea of using a book for a doll's torso. What followed was that Anne further experimented with using books and began introducing altered books in the dollmaking classes she teaches. Through these classes, Anne has opened a door that many other doll artists have entered.

ANNE'S THOUGHTS

Years ago, as an art teacher in a public high school, I taught many forms of paper and fiber arts. I left teaching for a full-time career as a contemporary basketmaker and, later, as a doll artist. Four years ago, I rekindled my interest in the paper arts. From there, it seemed a natural step for me to mix my fiber and art doll work with the paper arts.

In both dollmaking and altered book art, I've found that just about anything I use in dollmaking can be used in altered book art. As a self-taught dollmaker, I am free to try any technique and use any material to create the figures I design; there are no how-to conventions for doll construction to hamper my journeys into this wonderful fantasy world. I am free to express spontaneous ideas in assembling and refining my dolls. This freedom and spontaneity makes it easy to cross over into altered bookwork. In this instance, the combination of my two loves—dollmaking and paper arts—led to the creation of book dolls.

ANNE MAYER HESSE
Journal Dolls, 2005
Journals, wire armature,
fabric, clay, yarn

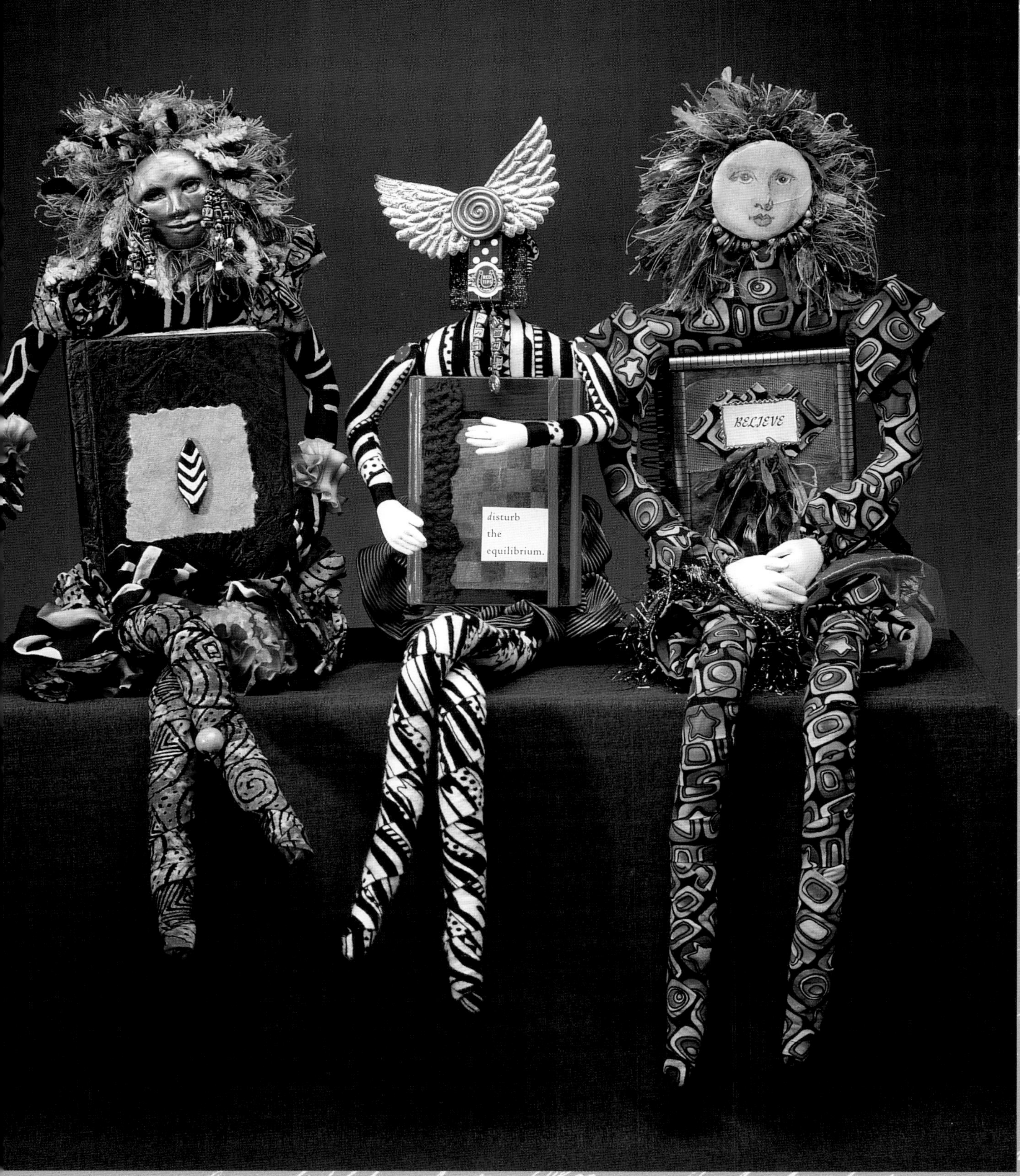
disturb
the
equilibrium.
BELIEVE

NICOLE MCCONVILLE,
ASSEMBLAGE ARTIST

Nicole's work recycles old books. Instead of considering an altered book as the end product, Nicole uses parts of books as elements in larger assemblage pieces. This adds a new layer of meaning to what an altered book can be. For me, Nicole's work stands as some of the most interesting work that uses book parts as crossover art.

NICOLE'S THOUGHTS

I love books, plain and simple. From my college literature studies and my occasional stint of journaling to exploring the creative possibilities of traditional bookbinding, I've always regarded books as a powerful vehicle for communication. I love the beauty of a well-executed binding, the musty smell of an antique find, the way books feel when I cradle them in my hands or lap.

Shortly after I started amassing a collection of vintage books on medicine, palmistry, astronomy, and other topics, I started to feel the need to explore the beauty concealed within their pages. The poignancy of a dictionary definition, the other-worldliness of an old illustration, the visual texture of printed text on paper soon became fodder for my assemblage experiments. Just like a cabinet of curiosities, each page unveils a world of mystery. There is something intimate about taking a book once treasured for its information and transforming it into another object entirely. Once I was able to see the riches between the covers, I soon found myself searching for new books to add to my library…and to my life.

*This particular piece, **Bare**, is a study in vulnerability and what it means to feel that protective defenses have been stripped away—literally and emotionally. My use of transparent layers of beeswax, sheets of mica, and anatomical illustrations helps echo that theme. The imagery came from a wonderful antique German medical book.*

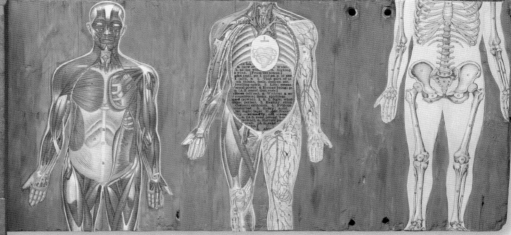

NICOLE McCONVILLE
Bare, 2003
wooden box, wooden scraps,
anatomical illustrations, found text,
dictionary text, feathers, mica,
beads, metal scrap, rubber washer;
painted, collaged papers, book
pages soaked in wax

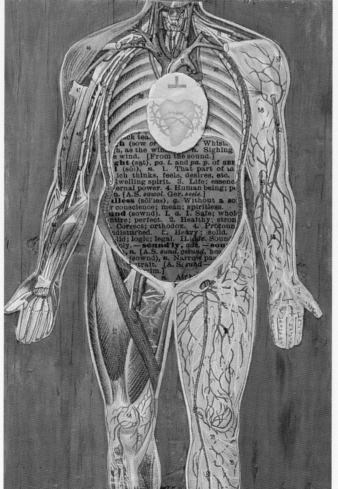

Printmaking is closely related to the book arts. For hundreds of years, prints were tipped, or placed, into printed book pages to provide illustrations. Even though printmaking consists of many different expressions—such as etchings, silk screens, soft block carvings, and woodcuts—there is a common thread: printmakers, like authors and commercial publishers, think of themselves as producing editions rather than a single work. With that in mind, I thought it was a natural step to see how a printmaker has crossed over into the world of altered books.

REBECCA ARANYI, PRINTMAKER

REBECCA'S THOUGHTS

From childhood, I have cherished books, especially the tactile experience of handling them while I was reading. Imagine my horror when buying a book for a college history class and I discovered there was no "book," just a CD! I had no pages to flip through, no pictures to leisurely peruse whenever and wherever I wanted.

This altered book, Destructive BookWorm.vrs, *is my reaction to that experience. I cannibalized a computer's CD-ROM drive that opens and closes to serve as part of the book. Mounted on the CD is a section of one of my lithographs; the shredded material is part of that same lithograph. I either wove leftover shreds in and out of slits made in the cover or made them appear as if they were "pouring" out of the book. I wrapped the shredded lithograph copies from the front cover to the back and then tucked them inside the book. As you can see from the piece's title, I had a point to make. My printmaking allowed me to put more of myself into the statement.*

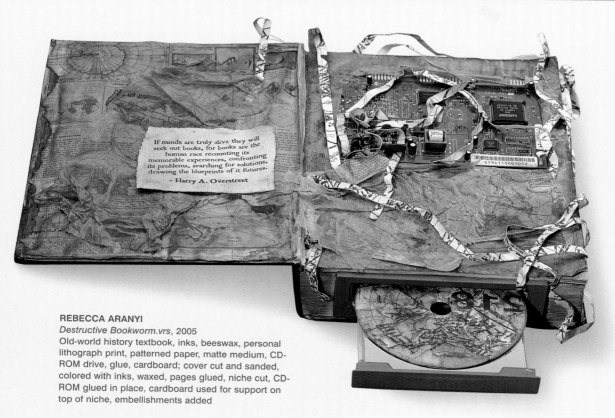

REBECCA ARANYI
Destructive Bookworm.vrs, 2005
Old-world history textbook, inks, beeswax, personal
lithograph print, patterned paper, matte medium, CD-
ROM drive, glue, cardboard; cover cut and sanded,
colored with inks, waxed, pages glued, niche cut, CD-
ROM glued in place, cardboard used for support on
top of niche, embellishments added

On the book page:
If minds are truly alive they will
seek out books, for books are the
human race recounting its
memorable experiences, confronting
its problems, searching for solutions,
drawing the blueprints of it futures.
— Harry A. Overstreet

Print! Using Image and Text

Ever wonder how an artist from a different discipline approaches an altered
project? Rebecca Aranyi asked printmakers who were unfamiliar with altered book
art this question:

"If I gave you a book (sized 8½ x 5½ inches), how would you incorporate your printmaking into altering the book?"

Here are some of their suggestions:
• Make small prints. Insert them in
  the book.

• Make a large print, cut it up, alter it, and
  insert it into the book.

• Show the process of color printing in the
  book. One page would have the reds
  from the image, another the yellows.
  Continue until you have used all the colors to make the print.

• Show all the stages of a woodcut,
  from a blank piece of wood to the finished piece.

• Take a poster of a famous print, and cut
  it up. Alter it in various ways. Emphasize
  different parts not normally emphasized.

• Take apart a book, and run it through
  the printing press. Use all of the pages
  by laying them down on the press and
  running them through. Then put the
  book back together.

• Cut holes in the book, and insert small
  prints in the holes—or weave a print in
  and out of the book. Have holes cut all
  the way through the book and just
  thread a print (approximately 2 inches
  wide) through the volume.

• Replace pages/chapters in the book
  with just prints, or make your own
  images for the story.

• Make a collage image from the pages,
  transfer it to a stone, and print it.

• Make collographs from leaves, gaskets,
  buttons or coins. (A collograph is a form

of printing that makes a collage out of
found objects.) Glue the items down
onto a surface. (Cardboard works well.)
Ink the items, lay your book page over
them, and brayer the back of your page
to create your print.

• Use glue to make a design on a piece
  of cardboard. After it dries, ink it and run
  it through the press.

• Use a mini-silkscreen, and screen-print
  all the pages. Book can remain intact.

• Cut out a square in the middle of some
  of the pages, leaving the last page
  intact. Add a print to the last page, with
  the outer pages acting as a frame.

• Use every other page as a stencil, and
  cut a design out while the pages are
  intact. Then print every other page,
  using the stencil page.

MARY ELLEN LONG,
ENVIRONMENTAL ARTIST

Colorado artist Mary Ellen Long uses her altered books both to dance with nature and to express her beliefs. For Mary Ellen, altering books is more than an opportunity for artistic expression. It is also a chance to take a stand and speak out about her deeply felt, strongly held values. Nationally known for her environmental installations and environmental books, Mary Ellen sees altering books as one more way to connect with nature.

MARY ELLEN LONG
Wrapped Book at Tres Pinos, 2002
Coverless books, like the two shown to the left and above, are wrapped with cord and left at the base of large pines. Each book tells a story of seasonal changes, animal presence, decay, and transformation.

MARY ELLEN'S THOUGHTS

I find strength and message in natural objects and sites in the mountain environment. The altered books shown here were a part of a series of bound books. Once bound, the books were left under trees. The four seasons joined with me to create these forms that speak of the slow process of nature: of growth, decay, and rebirth on the land and of our interconnectedness to nature. My belief in the power of art itself to affect transformation encourages my continuing search and journey as an artist.

Pamm O. Hanson,
Painter

Long before I even knew there was such a thing as altered books, I caught Pamm defacing an old volume. She was in a Seattle coffee shop, doodling, writing, and sketching over journal pages she had covered with gesso. It tickles me the ways Pamm paints herself: sometimes big, sometimes small. It all depends on how she sees herself changing. She is one of the most present and self-aware people I know. Her painting reflects that about her. Altering books is her secret activity.

Pamm's Thoughts

Altering books is a furtive practice and a secret pleasure that takes place in my studio. These books serve as my visual journal and my inspiration. They are intensely personal; rarely do I show them to anyone. I have the sense that it's the old books that find me at flea markets and tag sales. I paint, glue, draw, and even tear the pages. Text is sometimes highlighted or hidden.

So much of my studio life is "me painting me." My pages provide a lively dialogue when it is too quiet in the studio and a familiar refuge when it is too noisy. I especially love how an altered book can initiate a dialogue; the book can talk to me, and I can respond with my alteration. A book's bold shape and words make altering it feel like more of a collaborative effort.

The book pictured here was created entirely with found material. I rescued volume nine of a Funk & Wagnall's series, The World's One Hundred Best Short Stories. I found the watercolors in a bag in the garbage. My goal was to do a self-portrait; at least one a day, on consecutive pages of the small volume, using the limited palette of found paints. I didn't throw any result away. The old and dry pages would soak up the watercolor, demanding an immediacy of brushstroke. The materials were challenging, yet they created a ghostlike quality in the small paintings. This was every day of my life for one month: 51 pages, 48 paintings—all of me.

PAMM O. HANSON
Ghost Stories, 2003
Funk & Wagnall, 1927, The World's One Hundred Best Short Stories (Volume 9: Ghosts), watercolors found in trash; self-portraits done on consecutive pages every day for one month

JANE POWELL,
MULTIMEDIA ARTIST

I first met Jane through an artist friend who had discovered Jane's shop in Saluda, North Carolina. The store was, at first glance, a rubber stamp store. But I noticed that in addition to the stamps there was a vast array of art materials and an energy that screamed, "PLAY! INVENT! EXPLORE!" This energy is an integral part of Jane's own work as a multimedia artist. By constantly reinventing herself and using all sorts of art media in her work, she invites us to share her vision.

JANE'S THOUGHTS

I became fascinated with altered books about four or five years ago when Gabe Cyr taught a class at my shop. It was so different from anything that I had done in the past. And even though I was teaching my own students at my shop that there were no rules, I learned that altering books went much further than simply ignoring rules.

That first class paved the way to my grand adventure in altered art. Altering is my medium of choice now. I use books, pages, canvases, whatever I can get my hands on. I have learned that any type of book, material, and technique can be used in this art form.

A shrine book I saw in a publication inspired this canvas book. The shrine had no pages, just two stretched canvas covers hinged together. I thought to myself, "Yes, this is good, but what are the possibilities?" I decided that it could be a real book with pages. I just needed to find a way to secure pages to the stretched canvas. I began trying familiar methods and material combinations in order to bind the pages into book. Sewing signatures to an accordion-folded strip of linen book cloth solved my dilemma. I then moved on to creating the niche, and decorating, embellishing, and designing the cover. The finished project was a pure delight.

EXTRA PARTS

30 Paper-finger release arm
31 Margin-stop bar
32 Front rail
33 Rear rail
34 Escapement wheel

PARTS NOT NUMBERED

Front scale

JANE POWELL
Rationale, 2005
Pages and cover of old typewriter manual,
stretched canvas, mica, typewriter parts

JAN BODE SMILEY,
QUILTER

Jan is one of those souls dedicated to her creative life. She began her "artful" life as a quilter before turning her energies to stamping. From there it was a short leap to altered books. Now Jan's journey has returned her to where she began: working with fabric. "What if?" remains an important part of her creative life as she continues to search for new possibilities in her art.

JAN'S THOUGHTS

What I loved most about quilting was the layering: creating layers out of a fabric top, batting, and a backing. Color, texture, and pattern loomed large, but it was the building up of layers of these elements that fascinated me.

At one point, I was selling stamps for use on fabric. That led me to carving my own stamps, and that introduced me to the world of stamping arts and altered books. I was experimenting with layering and stamping on book pages, sometimes using fabric. I would grab a piece of silk organza and a needle when others were grabbing vellum and glue. The effect was similar, but different. After watching others work, I began using more papers, stamps, collage. I was straying farther away from my main art life and feeling a bit schizophrenic.

I needed focus, and it occurred to me that I could bring what I learned in altered bookwork and apply it to fabrics. I would paint, stamp, and collage onto the fabrics to create new visual stories.

The pieces here were created as I reintegrated my artist-self. They are quilt forms in that they are made from fabric and bound as quilts are. At the same time, they're a page spread, just as I would create in an altered book. I decided to build a frame to hang them on a wall. I like it that you can see the page spreads all at once, with each layered page hanging in the open, not hiding from the viewer behind another page.

JAN BODE SMILEY
Indulge Your Passions, 2003
Canvas, found objects, digital photography,
wood; painted, image transfers

JAN BODE SMILEY
Forest Floor, 2003
Canvas, wood; painted, stamped, stitched,
heat-treated Tyvek

JAN BODE SMILEY
Red Grid, 2004
Canvas, paper, metal, organza, pattern tissue, wood; collaged, painted

JAN BODE SMILEY
Favorite Days, 2004
Canvas, gauze, beads, wood; painted,
stamped, collaged, stenciled, stitched, dye-painted

LAEL ALON, GRAPHIC DESIGNER

The basic principle in altered book art is there are no rules. However, artists from other disciplines see this notion a bit differently. Lael Alon, a graphic designer, knows she can use almost anything she can envision to make a discarded book into art. But Lael also believes that if she doesn't follow graphic design principles, her finished work might be an enjoyable creative project, but it probably won't be art.

LAEL'S THOUGHTS

As a college student in the fine arts department, I grew increasingly frustrated about when to follow established art principles or break with them when those principles mostly seemed to be about subjective personal tastes. The eternal question for me became "why does this work and that does not?" If I didn't know the "why," it seemed pointless to continue.

I found those basic principles by switching to graphic design. Here I felt more comfortable. Not only did I have more clearly defined guidelines to use, I also began to understand how applying these principles to shape, space, color, images, and dimension could create order from chaos. With principles in hand, I become bolder in my artistic explorations. These same principles came with me as I ventured into altered books. I love weaving together graphic design and book arts. For me, they provide an interesting basis for creating my own altered books.

Part of the book's existing title, Soldiers, along with a prominent water stain that resembled flowers provided the inspiration for Soldiers of Pollen. I wanted each page to somehow relate to pollen, like my page that depicts sitting out on a beach, a place where you're susceptible to pollen attacks, or the page that shows a wall of glass windows blocking access to the pollen-filled outside world. I reveled in working with a three-dimensional object, something I am rarely able to do as a graphic designer who relies on a computer for creating.

What was the biggest surprise? It was the realization that working with multiple layers in the book was little different than the layering process in a computer graphics program, my primary artistic tool as a graphic designer.

LAEL ALON
Soldiers of Pollen, 2005
Found narrative; painting, collage

Surface Principles

Lael Alon suggests that if you're using type as an element in your altered book, keep in mind the following:

When placing type, make sure to put it close to the center of the page or near a strong visual element in the composition. If you place it near the edge of a page, your type will look as if it's running away from your book.

When adding type elements, try to stay away from large, chunky typestyles.

Blocks of type placed over a picture that has printed or torn edges does not work. The overall effect produces an image that appears sloppy and poorly thought-out. It can also distance the type rather than make it an integral part of the work. Instead, consider blending words into the book's surfaces by hand lettering in the spaces in between images or using the type to trace around an image.

RICHARD BABB,
PHOTOGRAPHER

Photography and books seem to be one of those natural pairs. So it probably shouldn't surprise us that we find photographers among the artists who are passionately altering books. They are the photojournalists among us, as we book alterers are the arts journalers. But the paths photographers take are many. Richard's work takes him down a path sufficiently different from that taken by others, and I wanted us all to really notice the possibilities he presents.

RICHARD'S THOUGHTS

The two things about altered books I find interesting are context and theme. The book becomes a context for photographs. This is something quite apart from the notion of placing photographs in scrapbooks to remember events or memories. An altered book presents its own theme and context. It creates new meaning by becoming a source of ideas to enhance or to contrast with the photographs. It talks to us. We respond with our art.

I love surrealism. I love the old surrealist tricks of randomness to get things started. I enter the book at random and let it talk and join in the joke I might be creating from its pages. Sometimes I begin with the pictures, and then look for the right book. At other times, I let the book itself suggest the subject of the photograph. It is a dance of contrast and support.

I also believe part of a book's beauty is that it is interactive. Marcel Duchamp believed that the artist never finished art. It becomes finished when the viewer looks at it. The viewer's perceptions finish it….so the art becomes finished in as many different ways as there are people who view it. So it must be in altering books.

Altered books are also portable, unlike the gallery wall. Where am I going with this? The altered book is altering my practice of photography. My photography alters books. Others see our dance. They finish it. Who knows what is next…?

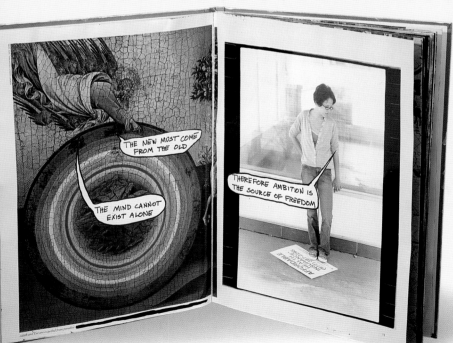

RICHARD BABB
To Love Life, 2004–2005
Conte, acrylic, liquid sealer, paper, pencil, pastel

As a photographer, I was looking for a way to present several snapshots that I liked—something more than a simple photo album. The approach was kept simple, and a working plan was conceived before I began the work.

RICHARD BABB
Rizon No. 1, 2004–2005
Photographs, glue, ink

I began this book using the old surrealist trick of random starters. I collected ideas and then began a series of photo shoots to get pictures that were specific to those ideas (mostly thoughts about western culture).

LynnDee Nielson,
Sculptor

When I first saw LynnDee's altered bookwork, I realized that I was not only viewing a well-crafted altered book, but also experiencing a powerful and deeply emotional expression. Besides being a book sculpture, this crossover work is a fine example of an artist taking a stand for something she believes in, a stand without rhetoric, and, in the process, she has created a powerful work of art.

LynnDee's Thoughts

I create art formed from the gamut of emotions felt during our lives. I draw on the human feelings of joy and pain and all their variations to build a visual metaphor that is both personal and universal. My art is a language built to communicate a feeling that verbal speech cannot. Whether that metaphor comes from altered books or from sculpture, each of my pieces contains its own structured language that lays open the content.

I define myself as a sculptor. I've always loved the feeling of drawing in free space. Increasingly, the number of dimensions I use pales in comparison to the message the art conveys. I create my work by starting with an idea and then looking for a medium that will best represent that concept, no matter what shape, dimension, or size. I am more drawn to organic shapes, shunning the hard-edged and geometric. Now I find the line between nature and art blurred, as my work has evolved to include more and more of nature's own art forms.

LYNNDEE NIELSON
Everything You Wanted to Know About West Nile, 2004
Vinyl three-ring binder, contact cement, acrylic paint, artist's canvas yardage, molding compound, wire and grapevine pages, poem about the diminishing number of birds, polymer clay bird; binder gutted and covered with artist's canvas yardage, inside built-up, carved, and painted

Sadness weighted me until I began working on this sculpted book. I have lived on acreage in Nebraska for a quarter of a century and have enjoyed sharing space with the countless birds that called this space home. Nebraska was severely impacted by West Nile virus; each morning, I collected the dead birds in my yard and burned them in my trash barrel. As the months dragged on, my bird feeders needed filling less frequently and the air grew quiet and heavy This book is my homage to birds—how I miss your song!

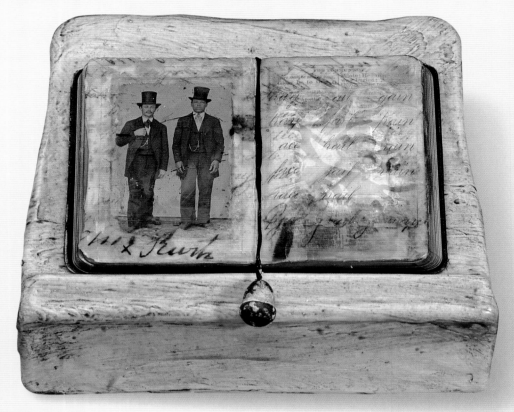

HOLLY HANESSIAN
Manipulated Man, 2002
Porcelain book stand, encaustic, collaged, found book, tin-type photograph, key, tape transfer text

HOLLY HANESSIAN,
CERAMIST

In contrast to photography or printmaking, ceramics and altered books hardly seem like a natural crossover combination…the solid hardness of fired clay facing the thin, fragile papers of the book. But imagining the possibilities inherent in that very combination brings us to the startlingly compelling work of Holly Hanessian.

HOLLY'S THOUGHTS
Why do I create art with ceramics and book forms?

The book, with its texture and visual structure, fills an important role in my artwork. The physical act of turning pages is similar to the intimacy created when holding a handmade cup. By combining these two tactile materials, there is a visceral connection beyond the ideas expressed in the artwork. I create sculptural objects, assemblage, and installations that combine handmade ceramic parts and found antiquated memorabilia. Old books, cradles, plumb bobs, body parts, and ceramic words all play different roles in my artwork.

For the last 10 years, I have been involved in either making books by hand or weaving them into my sculptures. Along with the words and stories they imply, these forgotten books add a sense of holding, loss, intimacy, and awareness. Old photographs, rusty hardware, and, most recently, ceramic words link the narrative structure together in the artwork.

HOLLY HANESSIAN
Henry Bobson's Daugher Sure Could Go Fast, 1998
Stoneware wall piece, embedded with text, old photographs, and mica, altered found book

HOLLY HANESSIAN
Ella Conjugates Love, 1997
Found book parts attached accordion style, stoneware pages imprinted with text, held together with metal spikes

KATE STOCKMAN,
WRITER

Writing is an important part of Kate Stockman's life. It is how she earns her living. In viewing her work, it occurred to me that writing is an important crossover form for many altered book artists. Kate's talent for the written word enables her to combine both words and images. The example of Kate's work pictured here illustrates the interweaving of images and words used to create her altered book.

KATE'S THOUGHTS

I love words. I find irresistible their origins, their meanings, their similarities, and their differences, even their appearance. I love reading and crafting a well-written passage.

I especially love playing with words. I am passionate about puns. I want my epitaph to read, "She finally came to her wit's end." However, sometimes playing with words is not enough. I need images to complete the expression. Once the words inspire me, I become relentless to find and create images to communicate my thoughts. My art helps me do that.

My altered art is also my shorthand. For example, while on a walk, I found inspiration in two pieces of nature: the first, a broken twig scarred with markings created by an insect's hunger; the second, a piece of bark with some sort of circular markings caused by insects or a fungus, and scattered on the inside of the cambium. The twig looked as though it could have held some ancient language carved by a long-forgotten civilization, while the bark markings resembled musical notes, another type of language. My mind started creating a story around these two pieces and their connection to the earth. Creating the book was a magical process, as I put real objects to words and descriptions.

Creating art (whether written or 3-D) is an intuitive process for me, a pool I dive into: clear, deep, and peaceful. I can feel a direct connection to the Spirit. That relationship allows me to become a conduit to create art. My hands may create it, but the energy that creates my art comes from somewhere beyond. Although this is a great mystery to me, I am extremely grateful for each experience.

The quiver was strung with
braided spider silk,
which she looped
over her shoulder
and across her chest.

Enora collected her protective quills
three of them,
a magykal number,
and tucked them, also,
into her delicate quiver.

KATE STOCKMAN
Preparing for the Journey
Old book covers rebound with artist's
story; mixed media pages

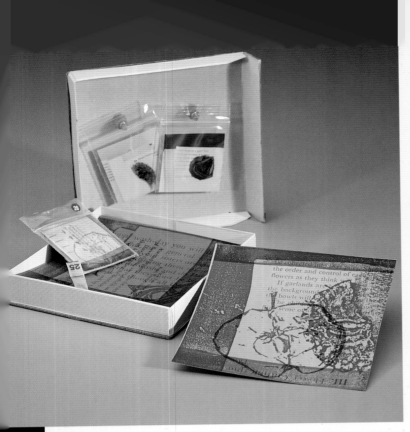

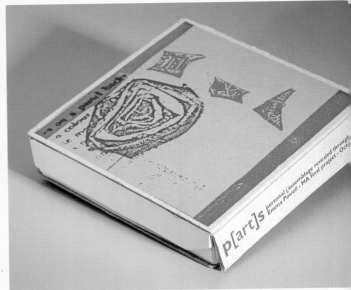

EMMA POWELL
Decay Prints Book, 2000
Salvaged video case, salvaged card, small bags, photos; screenprinted

These prints originate from close-ups of pages from an altered book on the theme of decay. The video case, which came from a local recycling center, was covered in an awful black vinyl. When cut away, a card cover was revealed that was ideal for screenprinting.

ELENA MARY SIFF
History of the Book Tower, 2003
Book about the history of the book; eight-fold books are stacked, windows cut out of each page, text applied around each window

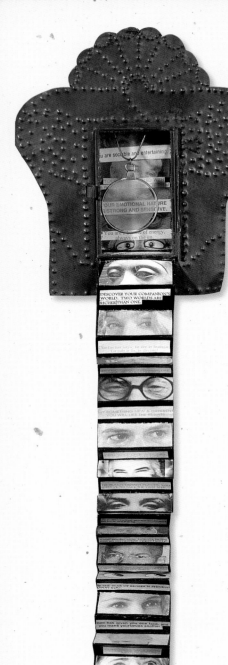

JAMES MICHAEL STARR
Neither Do They Reap, 2005
Collage, cord, antique buttons; left-hand page
tied to the front cover, right-hand page tied to the
back cover

This is my interpretation of a diptych in the form
of a book, as diptychs were two matching panels
that were among the first books.

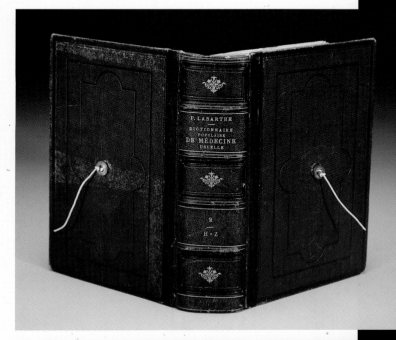

ELENA MARY SIFF
The Eye Book, 2002
Tin Mexican shrine frame, glass eye,
fortune cookie fortunes; eyes of
celebrities are featured on the accordion-folded pages; fortunes refer to
each celebrity

JAMES MICHAEL STARR
The Spectrum and the Light, 2002
Altered page

"After the Fall" is a series of collages based on steel-cut engraving portraits found in books from the 1800s. Each is enhanced with the addition of only one image from some other book.

JAMES MICHAEL STARR
After the Fall No. 21, 2005

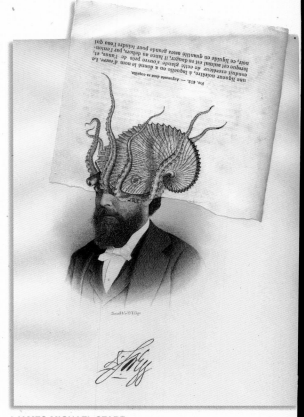

JAMES MICHAEL STARR
After the Fall No. 19, 2005

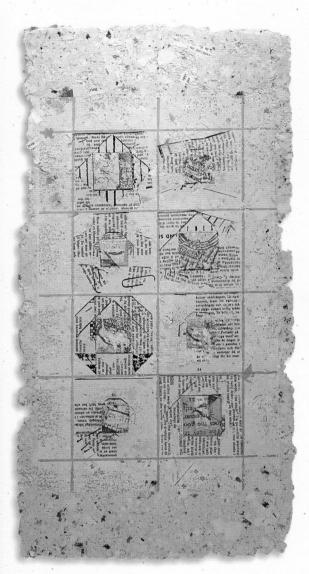

GAYLE WIMMER
Reconstructing Memory, 2003
1921 edition of *Webster's New
International Dictionary*, gauze,
beeswax

EMMA POWELL
Vandalised Print Series, 2000
Salvaged card, handmade paper from
salvaged book pages; collage, assemblage, screenprinting

MIRIAM SCHAER
Heart Control, 2002
The Atlas of Surgical Operations, girdle, dye, acrylic, glass vials, craft knife blades, needles, thread, linen cord

The Atlas of Surgical Operations, which belonged to my late father, is filled with detailed drawings and descriptions of surgical procedures. I was able to fill in the blanks regarding my father's mysterious work life. Typical of his generation (and profession), he was removed, and yet always present in my life. I came to realize that the processes of book binding and surgery have much in common: cutting and sewing to make something whole.

MIMI SHAPIRO
Neurotic Styles, 2002
Text book, dragonfly wings in plastic envelopes, pearls, empty antihistamine containers, lights, gesso, paint

In our society, with its materialistic culture, this book is a statement about how inferior a person is made to feel…unless they buy into the buying culture.

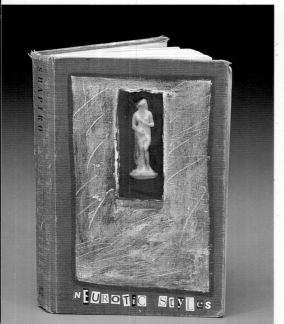

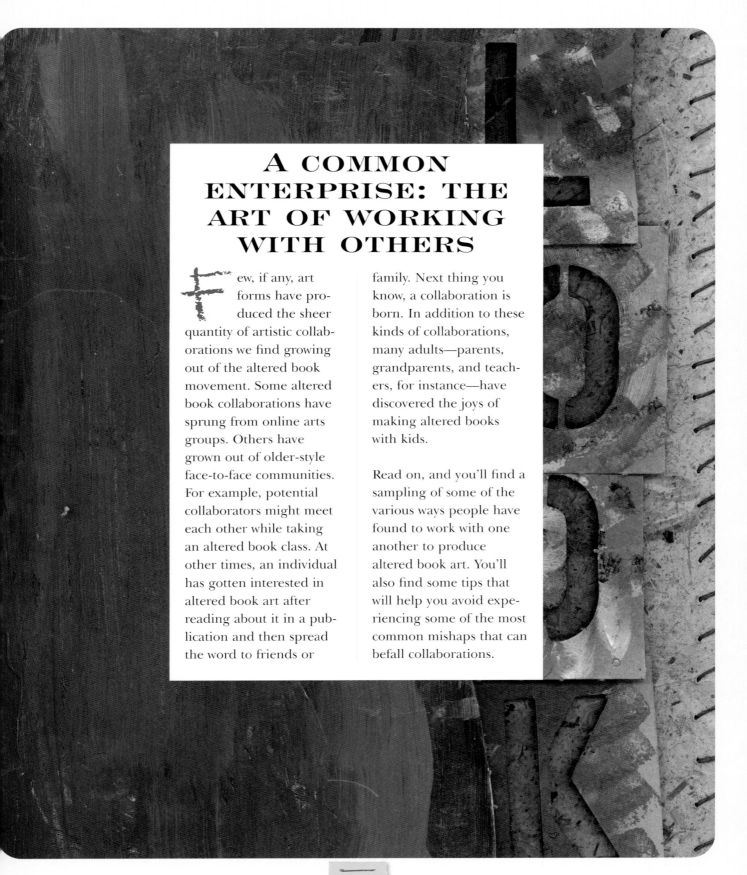

A COMMON ENTERPRISE: THE ART OF WORKING WITH OTHERS

Few, if any, art forms have produced the sheer quantity of artistic collaborations we find growing out of the altered book movement. Some altered book collaborations have sprung from online arts groups. Others have grown out of older-style face-to-face communities. For example, potential collaborators might meet each other while taking an altered book class. At other times, an individual has gotten interested in altered book art after reading about it in a publication and then spread the word to friends or family. Next thing you know, a collaboration is born. In addition to these kinds of collaborations, many adults—parents, grandparents, and teachers, for instance—have discovered the joys of making altered books with kids.

Read on, and you'll find a sampling of some of the various ways people have found to work with one another to produce altered book art. You'll also find some tips that will help you avoid experiencing some of the most common mishaps that can befall collaborations.

ROUND ROBINS

Online groups have really fostered the growth of altered book round robins. A round robin collaboration runs something like this: A group of six to ten artists scattered throughout the country, or the world, get together online and agree to do altered book art with a common theme. Virtually anything can serve as a focus for a round robin project: music, a color, a specific emotion, memories of an event such as a favorite trip, or even something as simple as a single word.

Charged with keeping everything running smoothly, the host establishes guidelines (see The Art of Collaboration, below). Then, usually, each contributor chooses a book and creates a sign-in page that serves as a record of all the artists who work on that particular volume. In some, though not all, round robins, the participant does the first alteration on the volume he or she has chosen. At a predetermined time, everyone sends the book they've been working on to the next person on the list. And so it continues until the book returns to its owner. Throughout the project, the host continues to coordinate the event by determining the timetable and rotation order for the circulation of books, knowing where all books are at all times, answering logistical questions, and occasionally mediating disagreements among members.

On pages 121 and 122, you'll find examples of work produced by one such round robin, a group of eight Southern California artists who participated in a 10-month project. In the spring of 2005, they exhibited their work in a show entitled "Fold, Spindle, & Mutilate" at the El Camino College library in Torrance, California, a rare opportunity to view, at one time and place, all the art created as part of a round robin.

The Art of Collaboration

We may think that there are no rules in altered book art...but there absolutely have to be rules for a collaboration to be a success. There is an art to doing altered book collaborations.

Round Robins

For any round robin to work smoothly, its participants must agree in advance on the answers to questions such as:

How much work is each participant expected to contribute to a book?

Are there any courtesies that need to be observed, such as not using perfumed substances or not smoking while working on a round robin book?

How much time does each participant have to contribute to each individual book?

How should books move from one artist to the next? In particular, does the artist need to follow specific packing and mailing requirements?

What notification should an individual send to the other participants when she's sent off or received a book?

What happens when participants' lives overcome them and they can't complete the art on schedule?

Professional Artists and Round Robins

Imagine a round robin that had our group of crossover artists (see Crossover Artists, pages 89 to 113) as participants. Because they must protect their professional reputations, there is a whole new set of questions that need to be considered.

Who owns the rights to the work in the books?

Who has a right to sell or display them?

Must each artist's work remain inviolate, or can individuals alter the work of the artists who've gone before them?

CALIFORNIA COLLABORATION

Complete set of eight books that comprise the
California collaborative project

Rebecca Caro's California Collaborative Book, Leslie Caswell's page

Rebecca Caro's California Collaborative Book, Noriho Uriu's pages

DAAL PRADERAS
I Dream, 2004
Appears in Noriho Uriu's California collaborative book

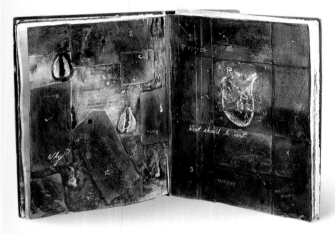

CLAUDIA M. MORALES
What Should Be Isn't, 2005
Appears in Rebecca Caro's California collaborative book

DAAL PRADERAS, 2004
Appears in her own California collaborative book

SERIAL ROBINS

A variation on the round robin is the *serial robin*. An artist with an interesting idea launches a serial robin by asking others to work on a project for the fun and challenge of it. In this type of round robin, only one book circulates among the participants. For example, Pam Yee, who has served as the president of the International Society of Altered Book Artists, initiated a serial robin that resulted in the dictionary pictured here and on the next page. After finding a dictionary with removable sheets, Pam sent pages to the participants, asking each of them to incorporate a definition from the dictionary page they'd received into his or her art. When they sent the pages back to her, she decorated the covers and then reinserted the pages into the book. It was then her art to keep.

These pages are examples of how artists interpreted various words in the dictionary. Of course, when you participate in a round robin or a serial robin, you take a chance. Giving your time and talent away to another's book does not guarantee that you'll receive great art back. Still, in taking that risk, you have the opportunity to learn how not to take yourself so seriously. You learn to trust that even if you give your good art away, you can always make more. You and your art are valuable, just not so precious.

Also, round robins allow us to learn from one another. We learn by actually holding another artist's artwork in our hands for a few weeks, closely

SERIAL ROBIN
Collaborative book project with a dictionary theme, started by Pam Yee
Clockwise: Pam Yee, covers; inside covers, Linda Engelhuber; pages, Rita McNamara; pages, Gabe Cyr

inspecting the art it contains. We can then use those observations as a springboard, one that inspires us to try something we might not have thought of on our own. I remember my excitement when the first round robin book I'd ever originated made its way back to me. A distant artist had colored about 10 pages, folded them into layered pockets, and stuffed them with interesting tags. Never had I seen such a thing, nor would I ever have thought of it. It got me thinking. I thought about what else might be fun to stuff into pockets or what other ways you could create them. For me, seeing others' work has opened up a whole world of possibilities.

BOOK ALTERING GROUP LADIES (BAG LADIES)
Collaborative book project with a gardening theme
Top: Meg Fowler
Middle: Denise Henderson
Bottom: Shelley Moore, right page; Meg Fowler, left page

OTHER WAYS OF COLLABORATING

Collaborative challenges have also flourished as a result of online altered book communities. These challenges can be as informal as one artist daring other artists to make an altered book spread using their least favorite colors. The participants then scan the art they've created in response and post it on the Internet for all to see. Challenges can also be more formal, as when each participant agrees to fashion a 5-inch-square piece of art each day for a month; each artist then actually trades the resulting artwork with the other participants. Regardless of whether the challenge is formal or informal, it always stimulates plenty of online discussion: What was most difficult about the challenge? What was most surprising? What has the challenge inspired its participants to try for the first time?

Not all collaborative projects rely on the Internet to operate. The Book Altering Group Ladies, or BAG Ladies for short, provide a good example of a collaborative project that grew out of a group that met face to face. These were nine artists who held monthly meetings free of charge in the Saluda, North Carolina, shop and studio space belonging to one of its members, Jane Powell. They gathered to share ideas and challenge each other to make experimental work.

To thank Jane for making the meeting space available to them, the group decided to surprise her with an altered book, one that focused on her love of gardening. (See the photos on page 123.) So this was a project that was primarily product-driven instead of process-driven. Spearheading the project was mixed media artist Meg Fowler, who determined the project parameters, such as the page size and due dates. What they produced was a gift that Jane cherishes.

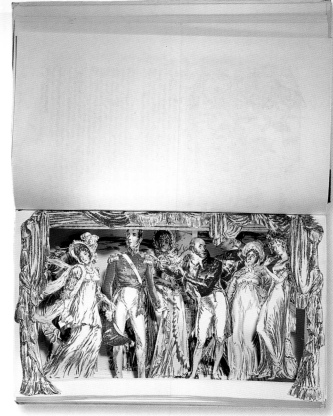

SOPHIA MICHAHELLES, *Vanity Fair*
Support provided by Maine Arts Commission, Maine Humanities

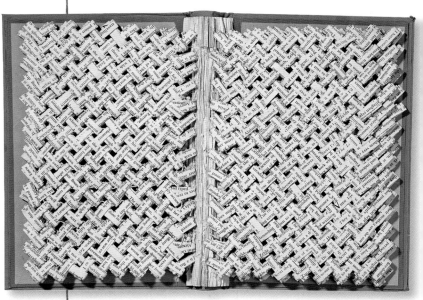

PATRICIA KACZMAREK, *Zelda*
Support provided by Maine Arts Commission, Maine Humanities

INSTITUTIONS WORKING TOGETHER

Another intriguing collaboration has recently taken place in Portland, Maine. If I had to pick two institutions with the most power to legitimize book altering as an art form, it would be a public library and a fine arts college. And those are exactly the two institutions that came together to create an innovative project.

It was the Portland Public Library and the Maine College of Art that came up with a simple yet extraordinary idea: create altered books that could then be checked out by the library's patrons. Michael Whittaker, manager of the public library's Reiche branch, had been thinking about the changing nature of the book. Specifically, he was convinced that even though we are in the midst of a transition to a future in which books as we've known them are being transformed, the book will continue to fulfill its essential function: serving as a means of communication. He talked about all this with a friend, Adrienne Herman, an instructor at the Maine College of Art. Out of their discussions grew the project that

SUSAN WINN, *Field of Greens*
Support provided by Maine Arts Commission, Maine Humanities

resulted in the four works pictured here and on the preceeding page. Instead of communicating through the words found between its covers, these books could continue to do so by being reinvented as art.

They directed art students to choose a book from among those already removed from the library system and turn it into an art piece. At the end of six weeks, the students turned over 180 altered books to the library. In 2005, the library and the college sponsored an exhibit of their work entitled "Long Overdue: Book Renewal" at the library's Lewis Gallery, with another show scheduled for 2006 at the college. And the library has made every one of these pieces of book art available to anyone with a library card anywhere in the country through interlibrary loan. So go ahead and shock your local librarian by ordering one of these books!

JUSTIN RICHEL, *Pioneers of Evolution*
Support provided by Maine Arts Commission, Maine Humanities

AMANDA CASWELL
Amanda's Book, 2004
Paint, ephemera, pastel; collage

WORKING WITH KIDS

You'll soon discover just how naturally kids take to altered book projects. After all, kids spend their days operating in the world of "what if?" You can do altered book projects either one-on-one with that special child in your life or with a whole group of kids—a scout troop, a home school group, or kids attending a day camp, for example. The key is knowing what children do—and don't—need from you.

What they don't need from you are any rules for making art. This always goes over well with kids, reports Sandra Hardee, who worked as an elementary school art teacher in South Carolina. "My students had never seen anything like altered books before," says Sandra. "They relished the 'No Rules' concept! Some of them forfeited recess to come to the art studio to probe my mind for ideas, to add something to their books that they had thought of during the night, or to see if the paint was dry." For Sandra's lesson plan, see How to Do Altered Book Projects with Groups of Kids and Still Stay Sane, page 128.

GRACE CASWELL
Astral Plane, 2005
Paint, beads, flower; collage

ERIC SUAREZ
Eric's Superhero Book, 2002
Children's board book; altered by five-year-old Eric Suarez

It's important to strike a careful balance, as Sandra does, between providing the structure, support, and help children need on one hand and letting the child drive the project on the other. The first step in being able to do this successfully is to know the child you're working with by watching and listening closely.

Based on the information you gather from your observations, tailor the project to the child's age, his or her familiarity with art materials, and the child's special interests. Gauge which tasks they're going to need help with. For example, if you're working with children under 10, you'll probably need to do chores they'd find overwhelming, tedious, and possibly dangerous, such as sanding or priming a board book, or cutting a niche. If the child can't read or write yet, they may well ask you, as California artist Leslie Caswell's four-year-old daughter Grace did, to write down a word they

How to Do Altered Book Projects with Groups of Kids and Still Stay Sane

Here's what Sandra Hardee, former elementary school art teacher, suggests:

Introduce kids to a topic—art, artists, nature, their favorite hobbies, writing, etc.

Set up a resource center of books and printouts that show altering techniques and a library of altered books they can examine.

Give them each a discarded book to alter.

Set up a workspace filled with art and writing materials, magazines they can tear words and pictures out of, and assorted ephemera. Make sure there is a place where their book can rest undisturbed while the kids wait for paint to dry, or if they've finished for the day.

Let them know when they'll be able to work: for example, two hours every Wednesday or all morning for one week.

Demonstrate a few things to do, like painting on pages, tearing pages out, or folding and gluing a pocket to tuck things into. You might want to show a new book altering technique possibility each time you get together.

Tell them there are no rules…they can do anything they want to the book. You are there to help if they can't figure out how to do something they'd like to try.

Notice what they do, and share your amazement at it. When they invent a new thing, celebrate it with them.

Set up a time for them to share with you and each other what they are doing or planning to do.

Just a bit before the end of altering time, give them a heads up that time is coming to an end: "Five minutes to clean up time!"

want to incorporate into an altered book. Her eight-year-old daughter Amanda, in contrast, is pretty self-sufficient. After all, when you're eight, it's about doing your own thing.

You can also show the kids some examples of altered books, demonstrate techniques they can use, and then give them access to lots of art materials. California artist Claudia McCain bought her seven-year-old daughter Gabriela a tackle box in which the young artist keeps glue stick, paste, crayons, watercolors, pencils and markers, glitter, buttons, patches of fabric, and small found objects.

"Gabriela came in my studio, pulled up a stool, and asked if she could use one of the prepared books on the table," Claudia recalls. "She immediately decided it was going to be an 'about me' book. She didn't work from front to back. Instead she approached it as she pleased. I gave her no help on her book, and she didn't ask for any." Claudia knew her Gabriela…and just stepped out of her way. She knew how important it was for her daughter to do the project herself.

I did a project with my artistically gifted, hearing-impaired grandson Eric. What I knew about Eric before we started was that he loved drawing superheroes and that those drawings inspired outrageous stories. I also knew that his art didn't tend to be very tidy or controlled, that he was easily frustrated when he couldn't realize his ideas—and that he had just turned five.

Taking all that into consideration, I planned a project in which he could paint wild backgrounds on board book pages with watercolors. Drawing first on paper with markers helped allay his frustration because he knew that if he didn't like how his art was turning out, he could just toss it and try it again. While the last of the painted backgrounds was drying, Eric decided on the sequence of his

drawings and dictated his story to me, which I then typed into the computer. He tore out the drawings, put them through a machine that made them into big stickers, and then pasted them onto the book's pages. We fit the story into the spaces he left between the drawings. After adding the title and a photo of Eric in a superhero costume, we completed his artwork, one that is, according to its creator, "way cool."

GABRIELA McCAIN
All About Me!, 2005
Crayon, acrylic paint, marker, watercolor, glitter, string, tissue, found materials; collage, drawing

Staci Allen's poetry on pages altered by Gabe Cyr in a collaborative book called *Ocean*

Some artists collaborate repeatedly.
These photos are the combined efforts
of Anne Mayer Hesse of the United
States, Jill Maas of New Zealand, and
Pearl Moon of Australia.

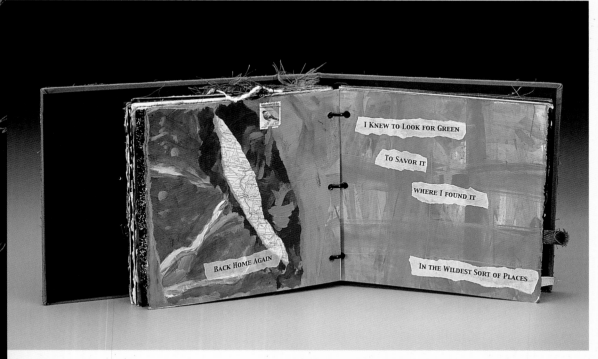

New Colors Round Robins: *Green* (Gabe Cyr's pages)
Altered photo album, paper collage cover, mixed media collaboration including fabric, fabric transfers, paint, collage, writing

This book, submitted by Vivian Montre, was created for a round robin project hosted by Jeannine Peregrine.

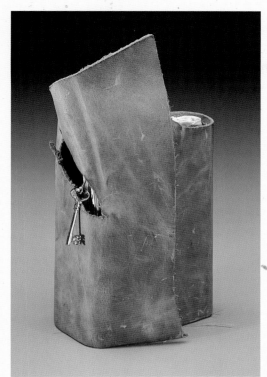

GABE CYR
Leather cover
SHARON FRASER
Mystic Journeys, 2002

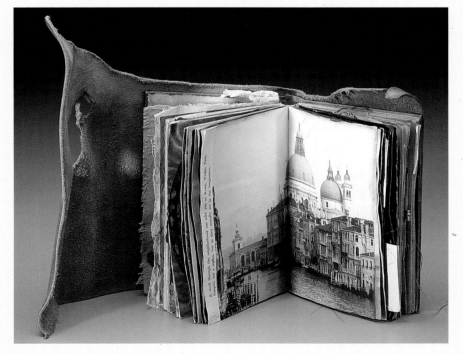

LEA CIOCI
The Reality of Art, 2004
Fabric collage image, quotes,
mica, water-color cakes, paint

ELLEN WALLENSTEIN
An Odd Collection, 1984
Paper, paint, photos, collages, text,
ephemera, glue

A box of pages…one page a day for 50
days, no skipping or starting early. A
diary from a life-changing year.

GIGI STARNES
In the Jungle, 2003
Miniature book, glue, paper towel to edge
niche, iridescent inks, dried grasses, tissue
paper, brass leopard; cut niche

SHARON MCCARTNEY
A Constant Sound of Birds, 2004
Altered vintage book; open with niche view;
gelatin prints, photocopy transfers, papers,
teabags, feathers, found objects, lace, bone
clasp; painted, drawn, stitched.
Photo © Marcia Ciro

JO ANKENY (cover) and **JILL MAAS** (inside)
The Listeners

VIVIAN MONTRE
Tequila Sunrise, 2003–2004
Hardback, mixed-media collage, ink, paint, rubber stamps, writing, heavy scrapbook paper, fabric cover with milagros, tin, beads, letter tiles; original spiral binding and cover used, with scrapbook paper added for pages

This was a round robin project, with an intentional color scheme of vibrant reds, yellows, and oranges and a Latin theme throughout.

LISA COOK
School Days, 2004
Children's textbook, glue, library card pocket that holds a miniature book created by scanning an old book cover and reducing the size, old file folder tab attached with eyelets

This altered book was part of a tip-in exchange, in which several participants sent me multiple single pages. The theme, "vintage school days," was particularly close to my heart, as I am a public school teacher in my other life.

Fig. 8 is the nose of a person who has no high ideals.

He will rush in where angels fear to tread

LISA KOKIN
Nose, 1997
Altered record album storage book; photo,
thread, textbook image; mixed media

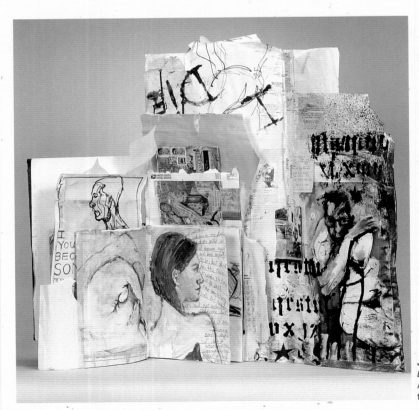

JULIANA COLES
Life Within, 2000–present
Altered book; figure drawings,
text; mixed media

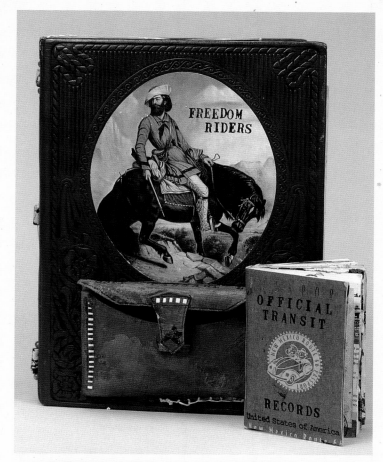

JULIANA COLES
Freedom Riders, 2003–present
Altered book; plastic, acetate, fabric,
found objects, imitation sinew, beads

Featured Artists

Lael Alon

In spite of her BFA in Communication Design from the College of Visual Arts in St. Paul, MN, Lael decided she is no artist. She considers herself a storyteller, telling her stories with the pictures she witnesses in her imagination. Those mind pictures connect discarded things, her own old art works, the imagined viewer, and herself as the artist to create something entirely new…a new visual story. Currently Lael works as a free lance graphic designer in Asheville, NC, where she also exhibits her altered art and other creative fruits at Woolworth Walk Gallery. You can contact her at laelalon@hotmail.com.

Rebecca Aranyi

Rebecca studies printmaking at the University of North Carolina at Charlotte, where she is seeking a Bachelor of Arts degree with an Art Education Teachers license. She is currently exploring different aspects of fiber arts, while constructing sculptures with a series of discarded chairs. Rebecca lives in Matthews, North Carolina, with her husband, three children, Lucy the wonder dog, and two ducks, Lou and Ethyl, who may be renamed Peking and l'Orange this fall. You can visit her website at: www.twistedfiberarts.com.

Richard Babb

This voracious reader of fiction and history is also an acoustical guitarist who met his wife while working as a restaurant's house musician. To support his art, photography, music, and family habits, Richard is a freelance commercial photographer and teaches photography at both a local college and John C. Campbell Folk School in North Carolina. Guess who made book altering part of the photography curriculum? If you can't answer that question, contact Richard at: tidwellbabb@charter.net.

Holly Hanessian

Holly Hanessian has widely exhibited her work and has been published in journals, magazines and books on the ceramic arts. She is a professor at Florida State University, where she heads up the ceramic program. Visit her webpage at www.holly-hanessian.com for current information on exhibitions, articles, and workshops.

Pamm O. Hanson

She's an easel painter, oil on canvas most of the time… always painting from direct perception, using her own figure and skin. She reveals her history as she paints her aging, changing body. The surface holds her memories, desires, and her culture. Subject and object, she too becomes one who has touched her skin. She lives and rides her horse in Washington state. You can contact Pamm at pammoh@comcast.net.

Anne Mayer Hesse

Anne is a high school art teacher who became a nationally recognized contemporary basket maker, and evolved into an internationally collected contemporary art doll artist and teacher. Now living in Kentucky, she continues her doll artistry alongside her love of the last five years, altered books. You can contact her online at www.anniedolls.com.

Mary Ellen Long

Mary Ellen Long is a Colorado artist who received fine arts training in painting and printmaking at the University of California, San Diego, and at the Santa Reparata Graphic Art Centre in Florence, Italy. Her current exhibition focus of book art forms and installations combines her spiritual expressions and nature. Her work can be viewed online at www.greenmuseum.com.

Nicole McConville

Nicole McConville is an artist with a background in correspondence art and collage. Her assemblage constructions reflect a passion for salvaging the found object. She has recently shown her work in the United States, England, and Germany. View more of her work at www.sigilation.com.

LYNNDEE NIELSON

LynnDee has exhibited her sculpture across the United States, and won the grand prize in an international competition of 3-D digital art. Her inspiration comes from her favorite vacation spot…home and acreage shared with her husband along the Platte River in Nebraska. Critters are a major focus there. Over the years, Lynn has developed a sense of humor while watching the deer eat her prized shrub in the spring or the raccoons eating the summer vegetables. Sculptures? They can be viewed on her website: www.artistree.us.

JANE POWELL

Jane's career as a successful Chicago mortgage banker ended in 1994 when she moved her artistic self to a quaint mountain community. In Saluda, North Carolina, she opened Random Arts, where she encourages play without rules and small classes to stimulate ideas and creativity… Random Arts is the store's name. To contact Jane, or check out her offerings, try www.randomartsnow.com.

JAN BODE SMILEY

Author, quilter, mixed-media artist, letter boxer, adventurer, teacher, mother, Jan is dedicated to really living this life. Author of *Focus on Batiks*, *The Art of Fabric Books*, and *Altered Board Book Basics & Beyond*, Jan lives with her family in Fort Mill, SC, and can be found at http://www.jansmiley.com.

KATE STOCKMAN

Back in the seventh grade, Kate Stockman won the prettiest book report prize for an embroidered fabric book cover. This was a sign of things to come: combining fiber arts, books, and the written word. Now with seventh graders of her own, Kate and her family live in Hendersonville, NC, where she creates her art as often as possible and loves every-

thing to do with books. Most of her full-time career in higher education and non-profits involves writing and designing publications. You can contact her at kstockman@mchsi.com.

FEATURED SIDEBAR ARTISTS

MCNALL MASON

Growing up in a family with two artist parents, McNall is now an entrepreneur. She uses and explores creative arts as her relaxation and a way to rebuild energies in a new way. Altering books has been part of that relaxation.

TERI EDMONDS VODICKA

Teri is an altered artist and realtor living in Bolivar Missouri, with Greg, her husband and their two daughters. Her lifelong passion for books, garage sales, and anything moth eaten, rusty, or yellowed with age, was given purpose when she discovered altered arts in 2002.

RANDE HANSON

Rande is a self-taught artist, working mostly in oil, acrylic, collage and assemblage. She exhibits her collage and assemblage pieces in a local southeast art museum, and her decorative painted furniture in a local antique mall. Her work has been published in Somerset Studio and Legacy magazines, and Zines. For more information, check out her website at www.thehh.ebsqart.com.

KRISTIN SMITH

Kristin Smith has found that her degree in anthropology influences her art almost as much as the childhood explorations of her grandmother's attic. She concocts art out of fragments of unrecalled memories that seem peculiarly familiar nonetheless. Kristin has a thing for threes, and has three kids, three dogs, but only one husband. You may find more of her art on www.flickr.com/photos/fngsmith/

CONTRIBUTING ARTIST INDEX

INDEX

Metric Conversion Chart
Inches to Millimeters and Centimeters

Inches	Mm	Cm	Inches	Cm	Inches	Cm
⅛	3	0.3	9	22.9	30	76.2
¼	6	0.6	10	25.4	31	78.7
⅜	10	1.0	11	27.9	32	81.3
½	13	1.3	12	30.5	33	83.8
⅝	16	1.6	13	33.0	34	86.4
¾	19	1.9	14	35.6	35	88.9
⅞	22	2.2	15	38.1	36	91.4
1	25	2.5	16	40.6	37	94.0
1¼	32	3.2	17	43.2	38	96.5
1½	38	3.8	18	45.7	39	99.1
1¾	44	4.4	19	48.3	40	101.6
2	51	5.1	20	50.8	41	104.1
2½	64	6.4	21	53.3	42	106.7
3	76	7.6	22	55.9	43	109.2
3½	89	8.9	23	58.4	44	111.8
4	102	10.2	24	61.0	45	114.3
4½	114	11.4	25	63.5	46	116.8
5	127	12.7	26	66.0	47	119.4
6	152	15.2	27	68.6	48	121.9
7	178	17.8	28	71.1	49	124.5
8	203	20.3	29	73.7	50	127.0

ACKNOWLEDGMENTS

I thank everyone who has ever touched my life…all of it has been part of arriving at the making of this book …from Grandmere Lydia's sewing scraps to Sandy's harping "You should REALLY write a book!" And in the final throws of despair that I could truly make it happen, my friends Zoe Hecht and Meg Greene Malvasi, who became guardian angels to this book's process. Some of you who are on this journey with me find yourselves in these pages, but if not, you are no less important. Thanks!

Gabe